Thomas Schirrmacher

Biblical Foundations for 21st Century World Mission

World of Theology Series

Published by the Theological Commission of the World Evangelical Alliance

Volume 11

Thomas Schirrmacher

Biblical Foundations
for 21st Century World Mission

69 Theses Toward an
Ongoing Global Reformation

Translated by Richard McClary

Edited and Revised by Thomas K. Johnson

Assisted by Bruce Barron

WIPF & STOCK · Eugene, Oregon

Wipf and Stock Publishers
199 W 8th Ave, Suite 3
Eugene, OR 97401

Biblical Foundations for 21st Century World Mission
69 Theses Toward an Ongoing Global Reformation
By Schirrmacher, Thomas
Copyright©2018 Verlag für Kultur und Wissenschaft
ISBN 13: 978-1-5326-5580-7
Publication date 4/17/2018
Previously published by Verlag für Kultur und Wissenschaft, 2018

Contents

Preface: The Reformation and the 69 Theses

By Thomas K. Johnson

When a German Protestant theologian decides to use the terminology of *69 Theses* in the title of a book to be published for the 500th anniversary of the Protestant Reformation, there is obviously a reference to Martin Luther's famous *95 Theses*, which were issued from Wittenberg, Germany, on October 31, 1517. So an important question is, "Exactly what is the connection between the new 69 theses and the old 95 theses?" This requires that we take a little walk down history's lane to discuss things.

There long has been a historian's debate about whether or not Luther really nailed his theses to the church door in Wittenberg. Public notices and invitations to academic disputations were commonly placed on a prominent door in the era before newspapers, but we should not worry too much about whether or not Luther followed all the customs of his day. And historians have also debated whether or not Luther intended to use his *95 Theses* to spark debates that would change the structure of Christendom. Whatever his intentions, Luther's theses came to symbolize the founding of the new Protestant or Evangelical movement, which Luther himself soon recognized had roots at least as far back as the efforts of Jan (John) Hus (1369-1415).

When I first read Luther's 95, the professor who was tutoring me insisted that I should read them in the context of the other short texts that Luther wrote in that era so that I could experience from the primary sources how Luther was progressively working out the theological and ethical principles that shaped the early magisterial Reformation. My professor said I should give special attention to the short treatises which Luther published before the end of 1520, by which time the content of classical Protestantism was taking its distinctive shape.[1] And then I would also begin to grasp why the Reformation was not merely a theoretical debate about questions related to indulgences; then I would understand why Reformation was also a history-changing force whose power extended far beyond its European origins.

---

[1]   My tutor was Dr. Ralph Vunderink at Hope College.

In his great retrospect on "The Expanding Effect of Christianity" in the era after the Reformation, Kenneth Scott Latourette, the pioneering historian of missions, analyzed the effects of the Reformation not only on the religious and moral dimensions of life but also on several other dimensions of western political, cultural, social, and intellectual life. About the religious and moral dimensions of life he observed, "Perfection did not come with the Reformation, whether in Protestantism or in the Roman Catholic Church. Not all the clergy, whether Protestant or Roman Catholic, were well educated or were of high moral character. . . . Yet the Reformation wrought distinct improvement, both in the areas served by Protestants and in the Roman Catholic fold. . . . For the rank and file of the laity the level of intelligent comprehension of the Christian faith was lifted by both the Protestant and the Catholic Reformation. . . . For the instruction of church members catechisms for their respective constituencies were prepared by both Protestants and Roman Catholics. Among Protestants the circulation of the Bible in vernacular translations markedly increased. . . . Most and perhaps all awakenings within Christianity have given rise to hymns and singing. The Reformation was no exception."[2]

Latourette then sketched some of the expanding effect of Christianity in the supposedly non-religious dimensions of life which came as a result of the Reformation. For some thirty five years I have found this sketch to be inspiring. He noted the post-Reformation beginnings of international law, the attempt to say that the relationships among states should be regulated by something other than military force (such as moral or legal reasoning), and with it the claim that there are moral norms, even if rarely followed, that apply even to decisions of whether one may go to war and how a morally justifiable war may be fought. In the political realm, Latourette continued, "When carried to its logical conclusion, Protestantism made for democracy. Its basic principle, justification by faith and the priesthood of all believers, issued in governments in which each citizen had a voice and possessed rights and responsibilities equal with those of each of his fellows."[3]

In the sphere of business and the economy, Latourette disagreed with the standard twentieth-century assessment of the influence of the Protestant

---

[2]   Kenneth Scott Latourette, *A History of Christianity,* revised edition, vol. II: A.D. 1500—A.D. 1975 (Harper & Row, 1975), p. 972.

[3]   P. 977.

work ethic, not because it was essentially wrong, but because it did not sufficiently recognize the role of renewed Catholicism in the rapid economic growth in the West during the post-Reformation era nor that some of this growth started before the Reformation. Nevertheless he summarized the nature and influence of the Protestant work ethic, "The Reformed faith made incumbent on all its adherents a kind of asceticism. It taught that every Christian, and not alone clergymen, should regard his occupation a vocation which he should pursue in response the 'call' of God. In it he should work conscientiously as in the sight of God. He was to seek to produce what would be useful for the community. He was not to be idle nor was he to spend in selfish or luxurious fashion the fruits of his labors. He was to make all he could, spend only what was necessary, and save the surplus, although giving part of it for worthy causes. This led to the accumulation of private wealth and so made capitalism possible. Moreover, while Luther followed the precedent of the Church of the Middle Ages and forbade the taking of interest, Calvin permitted it. This also furthered capitalism."[4]

Latourette continued to sketch the wide-ranging benefits of post-Reformation Christianity through social activism, including aid for the sick and poor, orphanages, prison reform, exalting the role of women, and promoting marriage (partly by having married clergy). This was paralleled by spectacular growth in intellectual life, including the natural sciences, mathematics, and philosophy, not to speak of the great growth of theology as a field of learning, all of which swirled together with growing support for popular education and the establishment of schools for all children.

Very likely, Martin Luther was not thinking about the ensuing holistic moral and cultural developments that would follow from his 95 theses and his related treatises. He was concerned about recovering the Christian gospel for himself and his fellow Christians. But already in these early works of Luther we see the crucial convictions that pointed in the direction observed by Latourette. Let me glance at the famous 95 and then rehearse some of those convictions of Luther which surround the theses, which will then shed light on Schirrmacher's holistic 69 theses on missions which are before us.

---

[4]   P. 979. Latourette also disagreed with Max Weber's understanding of calling in Protestant ethics.

The 95 Theses of Luther begin,[5]

1) When our Lord and Master Jesus Christ said, "Repent" (Mt 4:17), he willed the entire life of believers to be one of repentance.

2) This word cannot be understood as referring to the sacrament of penance, that is, confession and satisfaction, as administered by the clergy.

3) Yet it does not mean solely inner repentance; such inner repentance is worthless unless it produces various outward mortification of the flesh.

4) The penalty of sin remains as long as the hatred of self (that is, true inner repentance), namely till our entrance into the kingdom of heaven.

5) The pope neither desires nor is able to remit any penalties except those imposed by his own authority or that of the canons.

6) The pope cannot remit any guilt, except by declaring and showing that it has been remitted by God; or, to be sure, by remitting guilt in cases reserved to his judgment. If his right to grant remission in these cases were disregarded, the guilt would certainly remain unforgiven.

Later in the theses Luther continued,

11) Those tares of changing the canonical penalty to the penalty of purgatory were evidently sown while the bishops slept (Mt 13:25).

12) In former times canonical penalties were imposed, not after, but before absolution, as tests of true contrition.

13) The dying are freed by death from all penalties, are already dead as far as the canon laws are concerned, and have a right to be released from them.

14) Imperfect piety or love on the part of the dying person necessarily brings with it great fear; and the smaller the love, the greater the fear.

15) This fear or horror is sufficient in itself, to say nothing of other things, to constitute the penalty of purgatory, since it is very near to the horror of despair.

---

[5]   English translation taken from www.luther.de/en/95thesen.html. Confirmed 9 Feb 2017.

16) Hell, purgatory, and heaven seem to differ the same as despair, fear, and assurance of salvation.

17) It seems as though for the souls in purgatory fear should necessarily decrease and love increase.

Lest the terminology of medieval theology disguise to us the existential issues on Luther's heart, notice some of the key words in theses 13 through 16: dying, death, fear, horror, penalty, despair, hell, and purgatory. But then one phrase stands in shining, almost blinding contrast, "assurance of salvation." Luther's quest was how to find assurance of eternal salvation and freedom from guilt before God. And at the same time, Luther was deeply concerned that the quest for assurance of salvation and freedom from purgatory was driving people to inappropriate means, especially indulgences, which might lead to false security before God. And even if the popular sermons of the day were contrary to the complex theology of indulgences and contrary to what was taught by the hierarchy of the Catholic Church, it was what was heard by many an average Christian. In response Luther said,

27) They preach only human doctrines who say that as soon as the money clinks into the money chest, the soul flies out of purgatory.

28) It is certain that when money clinks in the money chest, greed and avarice can be increased; but when the church intercedes, the result is in the hands of God alone.

Luther's world was ripe for someone to step forward and say believers are justified before God and can receive assurance of salvation by faith alone in the gospel, not by indulgences or any other human activity. And a clear doctrine of justification transformed way the Christian life (and really all of Christian ethics) was conceived. To quote Luther's 95 Theses again,

45) Christians are to be taught that he who sees a needy man and passes him by, yet gives his money for indulgences, does not buy papal indulgences but God's wrath.

46) Christians are to be taught that, unless they have more than they need, they must reserve enough for their family needs and by no means squander it on indulgences.

47) Christians are to be taught that they buying of indulgences is a matter of free choice, not commanded.

With these simple lines, Luther set new priorities and standards for Christian ethics in light of justification by faith. Care for people in need is given pride of place; provision for one's family ranks far above indulgences; and a new standard is introduced by means of which Christians are taught to evaluate social institutions and practices, that which is "commanded," meaning that which is commanded by God in the Bible. Once free from the false security of earning or buying God's favor by means of indulgences or any other effort (such as taking inappropriate vows, especially related to a monastery), assured of one's justification, Christians are taught to turn to everyday life in a distinctive manner: loving those in need, caring for one's family, and asking what social institutions and practices are legitimized by being addressed in the Bible. The institutions of indulgences and monasteries were not legitimized by being addressed in the Bible, whereas marriage, family, and work are addressed in the Bible and especially in the Ten Commandments. So as not to multiply quotations, notice how Luther connected these principles in his 1520 treatise *The Babylonian Captivity of the Church*, "Anyone who has plighted his troth to a woman cannot rightly take a monastic vow. His duty is to marry her because it is his duty to keep faith. This precept comes from God, and therefore cannot be superseded by any human decree."[6] In Luther's view, monastic vows (and everything related to monasteries) are merely human decrees, whereas keeping one's word to a woman to whom you are engaged to be married is required because God requires truth telling and promise keeping in the Bible.

To grasp Luther we must see that he quickly turned from questioning the religious system of his time, including monasteries, vows, the penitential system, sacramental system, and indulgences, and turned toward explicating what he had found in the Word of God. And for Luther the key principle for understanding and applying the Word of God properly was the relationship between the commands of God and the promises of God, which he also called the relationship between God's moral law and the gospel. It was this principle, I believe, that led to the distinctively

---

6   *Martin Luther: Selections From His Writings*, edited with an introduction by John Dillenberger (New York: Anchor Books, 1961), p. 335.

Protestant type of cultural renewal and development in the lands shaped by the Reformation.

Luther's 1520 treatise *The Freedom of a Christian* illustrates his positive application of the Word of God, using striking rhetoric to both distinguish and connect the promises and the commands of God:[7]

- "A Christian is a perfectly free lord of all, subject to none."

- "A Christian is a perfectly dutiful servant of all, subject to all."

To explain this paradox Luther used language that sounded vaguely Hellenistic or dualistic, though his intent was neither Hellenistic nor dualistic. "Man has a twofold nature, a spiritual and a bodily one." The freedom of one's internal spiritual nature does not come from anything external; such freedom comes only from the gospel of Christ. "What can it profit the soul if the body is well, free, and active, and does as it pleases? . . . On the other hand, how will poor health or imprisonment or hunger or thirst or any other external misfortune harm the soul? . . . One thing, and one thing only, is necessary for Christian life, righteousness, and freedom. That one thing is the Word of God, the gospel of Christ." But in regard to one's bodily nature, "Each one should do the works of his profession and station, not that by them he may strive after righteousness, but that by them he may keep his body under control, be an example to others who also need to keep their bodies under control, and finally that he may submit his will to that of others in the freedom of love." Then when Luther talks about being a dutiful servant of others in the realm of the bodily nature, he frequently quotes verses in the Bible in which Christians are given commands to obey, in this case from Romans 13.

In one's internal spiritual nature, Christians should experience the freedom of knowing they are justified before God by means of trusting in the promises of God, by trusting in the gospel. Christians do not have to follow any external rules, regulations, or expectations to be justified before God. This internal spiritual freedom allows one externally to submit to the commands of God in submission to the needs of one's neighbors in love, to be a servant to all. Rather than being dualistic, this approach to faith and life is based on distinguishing commands from promises, the

---

[7] Dillenberger, p. 53. Subsequent quotations from this treatise come from pages 52 to 85 in the text edited by Dillenberger.

law from the gospel, a type of differentiation without dualism. "The entire scripture of God is divided into two parts: commands and promises. Although the commands teach things that are good, the things taught are not done as soon as they are taught, for the commandments show us what we ought to do but do not give us the power to do it." "When a man has learned through the commandments to recognize his helplessness and is distressed about how he might satisfy the law . . . here the second part of Scripture come to our aid, namely, the promises of God."

There is a distinct irony to be noticed in looking at the 95 Theses and the historical/cultural results of the Reformation. As of October, 1517, Luther does not seem to have intended anything resembling the results that Latourette so ably chronicled. Luther was interested in finding assurance of salvation, avoiding the two fatal distortions of works salvation or false security. But while mining the scriptures for answers to his life quest, seemingly by accident, in addition to a renewed understanding of the gospel, he also discovered a new understanding of ethics and society. Ethical life was not about purifying oneself or searching for new levels of self-denial. Instead he found a renewed motive for ethical behavior, love for neighbor; a new standard for the legitimation of social institutions, if they are addressed in the Bible; and a renewed view of the importance of correctly distinguishing while relating God's commands with his promises, relating God's moral law with the gospel. Thus, we can regard Luther's culture redirecting holism as accidental. In his younger years it was probably impossible for him to conceive of the possibility that his spiritual discoveries would change the course of history and nations. At least through the time of the 95 Theses he was mostly interested in eternal salvation and discovered the biblical doctrine of justification by faith alone; inadvertently he changed the direction of western civilization by his renewed approach to ethics.

This is precisely the difference when we turn to Thomas Schirrmacher's 69 theses. The inadvertent and accidental holism of Martin Luther's early years has become conscious and intentional. Schirrmacher's understanding of the Christian gospel is largely the same as that of Luther; what has changed is that Schirrmacher is thinking not only about eternal salvation but also about the culture changing power of the Word of God.

At first glance, one does not see a lot about justification by faith alone in Schirrmacher's 69 theses. Indeed, the term "justification by faith" does not appear at all in Schirrmacher's theses. However, it would be a terrible misunderstanding to suppose that Schirrmacher has left Luther's important discovery behind. To avoid such a misunderstanding of Schirrmacher, one can simply note what he taught in his studies on the New Testament book of Romans, published when he was a young man.[8] In these early studies we see how Schirrmacher closely tied the New Testament to the Old Testament, which is also an interesting characteristic of his missiology. While explaining Romans 3:21-31, a crucial biblical source for understanding justification by faith alone, he notes, "Righteousness by law-keeping, that is the claim that one can become just by means of doing the law, cannot be described as based on the Old Testament, for even there [in the Old Testament] faith came before righteousness, as Paul will show in Romans 4 by means of the example of Abraham. Righteousness by law-keeping is, rather, a distortion of the Old Testament. We Christians may not accept this distorted picture of the Old Testament and then set the New Testament against it."[9] About Romans 4 (the justification of Abraham) he notes, "Especially the promise to Abraham, and thereby to Israel, to which the Jews so frequently referred, is a decisive proof that righteousness is based on a promise and trust (faith), not on the law and its observance. . . . Paul concludes with the explicit statement that Abraham is not only a good example. What applied to Abraham in the Old Testament applies to us today (Romans 4:22-25), for the juridical foundation for our faith is the same as it was for Abraham: God-given faith leads to righteousness."[10]

Turning to Schirrmacher's theses on mission we find two distinctive emphases, the first on the Trinity and the second on missions in the Old Testament:

1) God is the first missionary.

2) Jesus is the missionary *par excellence.*

3) God the Holy Spirit is the most successful missionary.

4) The sending of Jesus' church is rooted in the fact that God first sent himself into the world as a missionary (*missio dei*).

---

[8]   The following quotations are translated from Thomas Schirrmacher, *Der Römerbrief,* 1. Band, Für Selbststudium und Gruppengespäch (Nürnberg: VTR & Hamburg: RVB, 1994).

[9]   P. 181, 182.

[10]   P. 205.

5) Since mission belongs to the heart of the Christian God and to the essence of the Trinity, Christianity without a concern for mission is unthinkable.

These first theses are brought together in thesis 9.

26) Mission is rooted in the marvelous eternal covenant of election among the Father, the Son, who died for us while we were still sinners, and the Holy Spirit, who was poured out at Pentecost.

These themes must be linked with how Schirrmacher understands the relation of the two testaments, the topic of theses 26 through 31.

27) In the New Testament, world mission is not primarily justified by Jesus' Great Commission but rather by the Old Testament.

28) The Old Testament rationale for New Testament mission shows that world mission is a direct continuation of God's actions of salvation history since the Fall of man and the choosing of Abraham.

29) The choosing of the Old Testament people of the covenant occurred with regard to reaching all peoples, such that world mission is already a topic found in the Old Testament.

30) For this reason, in the Old Testament there are already many examples of Gentiles hearing the message of God through the Jews and finding faith in the one true God. Moreover, many passages from the Old Testament prophets are directed at Gentile peoples.

31) Accordingly, world mission efforts cannot be presented and practiced independently of the Old Testament, the history of salvation in the Old Testament, and the destiny of the Jewish people.

32) The letter to the Romans also demonstrates that world mission has to rest upon healthy biblical teaching and that a healthy systematic theology always leads to mission.

It is worth noting that Schirrmacher sees the book of Romans as much as a book of missiology as it is a book of systematic theology which, in a manner familiar to students of Protestant theology and ethics, serves as key to a proper linking of many biblical themes such as the Trinity, law and gospel, Old and New Testaments. This leads to the holistic approach to mission found in his following theses which are much more consciously culture-changing than were Luther's theses.

32) The diversity of peoples and cultures is principally not a consequence of sin but rather desired by God. What is to be discarded from a culture is only that which expressly contradicts God's holy will, and not the diversity of human expression and lifestyle.

33) Christians have been freed from all sorts of cultural bondage. They no longer have to recognize human traditions and commands in addition to God's commands.

34) Christians can judge other cultures in light of the Bible when and if they have learned to distinguish between their own cultures, even their own devout culture, and the commands of God that are valid for all cultures.

What we see Schirrmacher recommending in theses 33 and 34 is what we saw Luther doing in his theses. Luther rejected many practices and institutions of medieval Christendom which he thought were not rooted in God's commands, including indulgences, priestly celibacy, and monasteries, based on a sharp distinction between his own devout culture and the commands of God. For Schirrmacher this is part of a culture-changing theory of missions, whereas for Luther it was part of finding assurance of salvation by faith alone, instead of finding assurance of salvation via the religious practices of his day. This culture-changing missiology is summarized in Schirrmacher's thesis 41.

56) Not only is the proclamation of the gospel to be formulated for various cultures, but the gospel should be enculturated in the life of each community and its entire culture.

The culture changing motif continues in several more theses.

56) The individual's peace with God, i.e., personal redemption owing to the gracious sacrifice of Jesus on the cross, is the first and most urgent goal of mission from which all other goals emerge.

57) Even if personal salvation is the first and highest goal of missions, that does not mean that there cannot be any wider objectives. Rather, all

wider objectives gain their significance from personal salvation. From inner transformation follows external transformation, and from the transformation of individuals comes change in the broader, symbiotic community.

58) Social work within the Christian church was institutionally anchored, from the very beginning of the New Testament church, in the office of the diaconal ministry, and this in light of cultural differences.

59) In Acts 6, social responsibility within the church indeed has central significance, but that does not contradict the centrality of proclaiming God's word and of prayer, which was institutionalized in the offices of elder and apostle.

60) Social responsibility on the part of Christians does not stop at the boundaries of the church.

61) The Bible is not a book purely for private edification. On the contrary, it repeatedly addresses many social concerns.

62) Whoever is in favor of diaconal work must also address the reasons why certain emergencies exist in the first place, as the Old Testament prophets did.

63) Human dignity and human rights are founded in the nature of human beings as creatures of God.

64) Whoever does not actively advocate for society to pursue a good and proper course intentionally or unintentionally accepts the standards of his or her environment.

One area in which Schirrmacher's theses seem to move beyond Luther and the Reformation is the central role given to religious freedom. One can wish that Luther's bold statements about Christian liberty would have immediately led him and his fellows to advocate full liberty of religion and conscience. But the Reformers were too much children of their age, which we still call the "Constantinian Age," to imagine the extensive separation of church and state needed to have freedom for several religions within one state. It took time for that conclusion to be drawn. That conclusion was drawn by Christians well before our day, though many Christians live in cultures were that conclusion has not yet been drawn by the culture and legal system. Therefore Schirrmacher theses on missions address this need in a section entitled, "Missions and Religious Freedom—Two Sides of the Same Coin." Here we find the following:

42) Dialogue, in the sense of peaceful contention, honest and patient listening, self-critical reflection, winsome and modest presentation of one's own point of view, and learning from others, is a Christian virtue.

43) Dialogue in the sense of giving up Christian truth claims or giving up world mission is inconceivable without abandoning Christianity.

44) Paul's address in Athens shows how good and important it is to study other religions and worldviews, including their texts, and to adjust the terminology and starting point of our proclamation so as to address the adherents of other religions and worldviews intellectually and linguistically.

45) Ethics and mission belong together. Christian witness is not an ethics-free space; it requires an ethical foundation so that we truly do what Christ has instructed us to do.

46) Gentleness is not only an inevitable consequence of the fact that Christians proclaim the God of love and should love our neighbor. Rather, it is also a consequence of the knowledge that Christians are themselves only pardoned sinners and are not God.

47) Mission efforts esteem human rights and do not desire to disregard the dignity of human beings. Rather, mission efforts seek to honor and foster human dignity.

48) It is reprehensible to bring about conversions through the use of coercion, deceitfulness, trickery, or bribery. By definition, such actions cannot result in a true conversion and turning towards God from the depths of one's heart in belief and trust.

49) Peaceful mission efforts have been essentially embedded as a human right.

50) One must differentiate between advocating human rights and religious freedom for adherents of other religions, or for individuals without any religious affiliation, and endorsing their truth claims.

51) Religious freedom applies to all people, not only to Christians.

52) Since the state does not belong to any religion and is not to proclaim the gospel but rather desires what is good and just for all people, and because God has granted human dignity to all people since he has created everyone (Genesis 1:26–27; 5:1), Christians should work together with the adherents of all religions and worldviews for the good of society, to the extent that other groups allow this and reciprocate.

53) The task of the state is to protect worldly justice, including religious freedom, not to promote our religion.

Freedom of religion is one of the results that should eventually flow from the proclamation of the biblical message. In an age of extreme religious persecution joined with widespread religious extremism and religious nationalism, this merits extensive mention in our missiology.

So I invite you to read Schirrmacher's 69 modern theses in light of Luther's 95 historic theses, linking the Reformation with twenty-first century missiology. I see the quest for assurance of eternal salvation as initially having unintentional but real culture-changing effects as Luther mined the Bible for answers; further mining of the Bible shows that the impact of the Word of God on society and culture should become intentional and conscious within our understanding of God's mission and ours.

Biblical Foundations for 21st Century World Mission

69 Theses Toward an Ongoing Global Reformation

By Thomas Schirrmacher

SECTION I: WORLD MISSION IS PART OF THE ESSENCE OF CHRISTIANITY

1. God is the first missionary.

God was the first missionary. He spoke of judgment, but also of grace. Immediately after the Fall of man, when humanity's history already appeared doomed, God did not leave things as they were. Rather, in his grace he himself came into the Garden of Eden to search for Adam and Eve and to ask, "Where are you?" (Genesis 3:9). Like every good missionary, God was not deterred by the fact that humanity did not want to hear the good news. He proclaimed judgment to them, and then he proclaimed the coming redemption (Genesis 3:14–21).

If a missionary is someone who brings the message of judgment and God's gracious answer for that judgment to people, not all of whom want

Translated from the German, first published as "Biblische Grundlagen evangelikaler Missiologie" in five parts in *Evangelikale Missiologie* vol. 30 (2014) 4: 171-183 and vol. 31 (2015) 1: 3-8; 2: 60-673; 115-121, published for the 30th anniversary of this journal and in the year remembering the 500 years anniversary of the Reformation. They are a largely revised version of the thesis published on the 10th anniversary of the journal in *Evangelikale Missiologie* 10 (1994) 4: 112-120 (numerous reprints). The Dutch version is found in "Bijbelse Principes van evangelische Missiologie." *Informatie Evangelische Zendings Alliantie* 26 (1995) 5 (Oct/Nov): 20-21 + 6 (Dec/Jan): 21-22 + 27 (1996) 1 (Feb/Mar): 18-20 + 2 (Apr/May): 24-26 + 3 (Jun/Jul): 19-20 + 4 (Aug/Sep): 20-21 + 5 (Oct/Nov): 21-22 + 6 (Dec/Jan): 20-21. English version in: Thomas Schirrmacher. *God Wants You to Learn, Labour and Love*. Reformatorischer Verlag Beese: Hamburg, 1999.

to hear it (John 1:11: "He came to that which was his own, but his own did not receive him"), then God himself is and was the first missionary.

2. Jesus is the missionary *par excellence.*

God the Father sent Jesus to earth as a human being so that he could take humanity's punishment on himself at the cross, in order both to effect and to proclaim salvation. Before the creation of the world, God had already decided (Ephesians 1:4) not to leave people to their self-imposed fate (John 3:16), but rather to send himself in Jesus as a missionary into the world (John 3:16).

3. God the Holy Spirit is the most successful missionary.

The sending of the Spirit is linked to Jesus as well as to the Father. The Spirit is the Father's pledge to his Son: "Exalted to the right hand of God, he has received from the Father the promised Holy Spirit and has poured out what you now see and hear" (Acts 2:33). Regarding the Holy Spirit, Jesus said, "When he comes, he will convict the world of guilt in regard to sin and righteousness and judgment" (John 16:8). The Holy Spirit participates in each conversion and is thus more successful than even the best-known human evangelist.

4. The sending of Jesus' church is rooted in the fact that God first sent himself into the world as a missionary (*missio dei*).

God the Father has sent his Son and his Spirit as the first missionaries. Foreseeing what was ahead, God spoke of the resurrection of the Christ, stating that he was not abandoned to the grave, nor did his body see decay. The Spirit remains the most successful missionary, and the church is only continuing the mandate in parallel fashion by going out into the world in mission. That is the reason for the existence of the New Testament church. Christian mission is unthinkable without the Triune God himself, without God as the one sending, and without God, in the Persons of the Son and of the Holy Spirit, as being sent.

In the New Testament, Jesus' sending of the apostles is understood as the direct continuation of the sending of Jesus by his Father (Matthew 10:40; Mark 9:37; Luke 10:16; Acts 3:20, 26; about 50 times in John, initially in John 3:17; compare Isaiah 48:16) and the sending of the Holy Spirit by the Father and Jesus (Father and Son are mentioned in John 14:26; 15:26; the Son is mentioned alone in Luke 24:49). In John 17:18, Jesus says to his Father, "As you sent me into the world, I have sent them into the world." In John 20:21, he turns this into a personal address to his disciples: "As the Father has sent me, I am sending you."

To begin with, *missio dei* means that God himself first of all becomes a missionary before he commissions people as his missionaries. Thus, God is not only always the sender, but also the one sent. *Missio dei* also means that this was not only historically the case in the Fall of man, in the sending of Jesus, or in the sending of the Spirit; rather, God in the Holy Spirit also remains the actual missionary, the one sent.

5. Since mission belongs to the heart of the Christian God and to the essence of the Trinity, Christianity without a concern for mission is unthinkable.

A presentation of the Christian teaching on God (referred to as "the doctrine of God") without a presentation of *missio dei* is not possible. Whoever wants to construct a form of Christian belief without a concern for mission must construct another God than the Father, who has revealed himself and still reveals himself in Christ and through the Holy Spirit. Theology is always missional because the God of whom it speaks is missional.

6. Jesus chose the twelve disciples/apostles specifically to prepare them for the task of world missions.

Jesus chose the apostles "that they might be with him and that he might send them out to preach" (Mark 3:13-16). Their intensive training through living with and working alongside Jesus thus prepared them for fulfilling the Great Commission once they were sent out on their own. The training that they received from the missionary *par excellence*, Jesus Christ, did not happen randomly and casually, but according to Jesus' conscious plan. This primarily becomes clear by the fact that (1) Jesus first of all solely proclaims, (2) then proclaims while his disciples observe, (3) then lets his disciples proclaim while he observes, (4) subsequently sends his disciples out for a limited time on their own and talks about their experience when they return, (5) and finally he sends them out completely on their own, though as the ascended Lord he naturally stays with them (Matthew 28:20). The disciples subsequently began to do the same thing with other Christians. The first, limited sending is reported in Matthew 10:1–11:1, Mark 6:7–13, and Luke 9:1–6. Jesus "sent out" (Matthew 10:5) and "sent them out two by two" (Mark 6:7). Given this example, the training of disciples in the direction of independence is a central element of mission.

7. Jesus' most important concern between his resurrection and his ascension was world mission.

With respect to the time between Jesus' resurrection and his ascension, all four evangelists primarily communicate complementary justifications for mission and commands to conduct world mission as the mandate that the disciples received (above all Matthew 28:16–20; Mark 16:15–20; John 20:10–23, especially 21–23; Luke 24:13–53, especially 44–49; Acts 1:4–11). Jesus' various recorded statements demonstrate that during this period of time, he proclaimed world mission in constantly new forms as the most important result of his suffering, death, and resurrection.

8. Christianity worships its founder in the same way as God himself.

Jesus is not only the originator or re-discoverer of metaphysical and ethical teachings for the church, like Buddha or Confucius. He is also not only the one sent to receive revelation from a God who reveals himself, like Moses or Mohammed. And he is not only an incarnation of the Lord of the world who proclaims divine wisdom, like Krishna. Rather, he is all these things together and, beyond that, he is God himself. He is, through his birth, death on the cross, resurrection, and ascension, the focal point and the turning point of world history and also the goal of world history, in that he is the judge of the world in the last (final) judgment.

9. Mission is rooted in the marvelous eternal covenant of election among the Father, the Son, who died for us while we were still sinners, and the Holy Spirit, who was poured out at Pentecost.

God's eternal decree to elect people to salvation, people to whom he applies salvation by the Holy Spirit and for whom salvation has been accomplished by Christ, has its source and foundation in God alone (John 6:37, 44; Ephesians 1:4); Father, Son, and Holy Spirit joined together in a missionary covenant. The motivation is God's own love, his eternal mercy, and his own glory. (Exodus 19:4–5; Hosea 11:1–4; Jeremiah 31:3). For us humans this remains mysterious, far beyond our understanding, but a proof of his unearned grace. The missionary covenant of God is not only a matter of his covenant people; it also has to do with individuals (Matthew 22:14; John 15:19; Romans 8:29; 9:13–22) whom God has chosen for a particular purpose (Isaiah 43:20–21; 45:4).

The Bible contains innumerable texts indicating that God plans all events from eternity and not only those that are good. Rather, evil cannot happen without his assent (Isaiah 45:5–6; Lamentations 3:37–38; the entire book of Job). This also relates to salvation, for God pardons those whom he chooses (2 Thessalonians 2:13–14; 2 Timothy 2:10). At the same time, many Bible passages speak about individuals' personal responsibility for their life and salvation (Deuteronomy 30:15; John 5:40; Hebrews 4:2) or about the responsibility of entire peoples. Today, in all Christian denominations there is a growing recognition that these two truths are not mutually exclusive but rather complementary. After all, the Bible often addresses both of them in the same breath (John 6:37; Philippians 2:12–13; Ephesians 2:8–10; 1 Corinthians 15:10).

10. Pentecost makes it clear that world mission in the power of the Spirit is the most important mark of Jesus' church.

Jesus instructed the disciples repeatedly to wait until the Holy Spirit came before beginning their mission to all people (Mark 16:15–20; Acts 1:4–11). The Holy Spirit was to come in the place of Jesus to convince the world of the gospel (John 16:7–11). When the Holy Spirit fell upon his church, both the New Testament church and world mission began. On the day of Pentecost (Acts 2:1–40), speaking in tongues and the miracle of understanding on the part of hearers from all parts of the Roman Empire made it clear that the gospel in the power of the Holy Spirit transcends all language and cultural barriers.

Acts 1:8 clarifies what mission looks like: "But you will receive power when the Holy Spirit comes on you; and you will be my witnesses in Jerusalem, and in all Judea and Samaria, and to the ends of the earth." Who conducts world mission? Jesus (Matthew 16:18) and the Holy Spirit (Acts 1:8). It cannot occur without the Spirit of God. The Holy Spirit will "convict the world" (John 16:8). The Holy Spirit is the guarantor of mission. If Pentecost had never happened, there would be no world mission. Reference to Pentecost does not mean an individual should overstep proper boundaries and limitations. Rather, Pentecost means God's Spirit has begun his work of world mission and has brought people into that activity.

11. Without the Holy Spirit, every form of world mission and every mission strategy are doomed to fail.

Only the Holy Spirit can convict people of their sin (John 16:7–10), lead people to the knowledge of God and of the saving work of Jesus, and make them new people in Christ (John 3:5). Even if God enlists Christians for work in world mission and wants them to use their intellect to reach others (consider, for example, Paul's many detailed travel plans and his general strategy, as described in Romans 1 and 15 or in 1 Corinthians), all such mission strategies are under the caveat of tentativeness, because God alone decides whether they will lead to success (1 Corinthians 12:4–6; Romans 1:13).

12. The topic of the history of salvation and of personal history with God is that God comes near to us. Herein lies a significant difference between Christianity and Islam.

In Christian faith, God in his revelation comes "near" to people (Ephesians 2:13, 17; cf. Hebrews 4:16). He comes to people, speaks with people in a language that they can understand, and gives the relationship between God and man a sustainable foundation by binding himself to his word as the one who is absolute faithfulness and enables authentic faith and trust. Precisely for this reason, the continuing revelation of God in salvation history edges toward a written version that makes reliability more palpable and brings it closer to all people through human language.

For its part, written revelation again moves toward fulfillment in a manner in which God comes *even closer* to us. God became human in Christ and made his dwelling among us (John 1:14). In Christ, God is Immanuel, "God with us" (Matthew 1:23). For that reason, the incarnation of God in Jesus does not suspend the written revelation. Rather, it fulfills it as the actual Word of God.

And yet, even that is not enough! God wants to come even closer to us. After the resurrection, Jesus, who is true man and true God, left the earth with his new body and sent in his place the Holy Spirit (John 16:7–11), who can come closer to all of humanity than Jesus could. Since Pentecost, the Spirit lives in all believers, testifies to their spirits (Romans 8:16; cf. Romans 9:1), and gives them internal power to live according to the will of God (Romans 8:3–4). God cannot come closer to us than that!

13. Though the individual side of the relationship to God is important, there is no such thing as lone-ranger Christianity. Rather, one is a Christian in community with Christ and his body, the church—i.e., with all our brothers and sisters.

On one hand, it is true that an individual should not be showy in displaying his faith. Rather, the individual should pray to the Father privately (Matthew 6:6). On the other hand, at the end of the Bible there is a formidable picture of a vast flock worshiping God together (Revelation 7:9–10). So, on one side, it can be seen that the Holy Spirit fills the individual (Ephesians 3:16; 1 Corinthians 3:16; Romans 15:13), but also the Holy Spirit fills the entire church (Ephesians 2:21–22; 4:4) and simultaneously assigns to all believers the gifts of the Spirit. The result is that together they serve to benefit the church (1 Corinthians 12:7, in the context of 12:1–13; Ephesians 4:11–13; 1 Peter 4.12–13). The individual nature of being a Christian is inseparably bound with service to a community, in which we carry out our joint service for and with God.

The complementarity of personal faith and affiliation with a local church congregation and the worldwide body of Christ should not be rendered asunder.

14. The fruit of mission, and God's chosen tool of mission, is the body of Christ, the church, and indeed the universal church of Jesus as well as the local church, according to the New Testament example of an organized church congregation.

For this reason, the church carries many honorable and high designations. It is, for instance, the "bride" of Christ (Revelation 19:7; 21:2, 9). Indeed, it is "the church of the living God, the pillar and foundation of the truth" (1 Timothy 3:15).

Christ's church, visibly assembled in its local form, which together praises God and is also active in the world, is indispensable for mission. With regard to the very first local church in Christian history, one reads: "They devoted themselves to the apostles' teaching and to the fellowship, to the breaking of bread and to prayer" (Acts 2:42). This same church established the first diaconate as a means of fighting poverty (Acts 6:1–5). And Hebrews 10:24–25 justifies the necessity of Christians' having regular fellowship with other Christians: "And let us consider how we may spur one another on toward love and good deeds. Let us not give up meeting together ..." The church teaches, exhorts, and consoles.

15. Christian theological training of leading workers is rooted in the training of the disciples of Jesus or Paul's workers to become missionaries and inspiring church leaders; for that reason, God's mission must be seen as the foundation, motivation, and goal of theological training.

The church cannot present and pursue special theology (the doctrine of God) nor theology in the broadest sense without placing the *missio dei* in the center, which both transcends and unifies all topics and questions to be studied. For this reason, theological training has to be missional and can never be purely theoretical. Theological training should motivate and equip future leaders for the present implementation of the kingdom of God.

Jesus chose the apostles "that they might be with him and that he might send them out to preach" (Mark 3:14). Their intensive fellowship with and dependence upon Jesus had as its goal their being sent out as missionaries. The disciples were not meant to always live in close fellowship with Jesus. Rather, they were to continue Jesus' mandate independently. Theological training also has to have sending and the Great Commission in mind, just as Jesus always had these same goals before his eyes when training the disciples (Theses 6 and 7).

Jesus' training of the disciples (Thesis 6) finds its continuation in Paul's discipling of fellow workers and the first church leaders. The letters to the Thessalonians are the best witness to the fact that Paul, and more specifically Paul and his co-workers (at that point Silas and Timothy; see 1 Thessalonians 1:1), not only proclaimed "simply with words" (1 Thessalonians 1:5) and communicated "the gospel of God" (1 Thessalonians 2:8) but were also prepared "to share ... our lives as well" (1 Thessalonians 2:8).

Training through living together and through intensive cooperation within a small group is not limited to the cases of Jesus and Paul. Rather, this approach was understood as programmatic and is documented in 2 Timothy 2:2, where Paul described his discipling and his training of future leaders as a continuing program: "And the things you have heard me say in the presence of many witnesses entrust to reliable men who will also be [or: should also be] qualified to teach others." This is a command as to how co-workers are to be trained. Training must assist those trained to become independent, not promoting long-term dependence on their trainer.

16. The spiritual success of world mission as the result of the invisible Lordship of Jesus Christ has been guaranteed and does not rest upon human activities or the condition of the church. The spiritual success of world mission attests to the Lordship of Jesus.

In the Great Commission according to Matthew, Jesus justifies world mission by saying, "All authority in heaven and on earth has been given to me" (Matthew 28:18) and that he would always be with his church (Matthew 28:20). The Great Commission is for that reason not only a command. Rather, it is also a promise, even a prophecy. Jesus himself will ensure that all peoples become followers, for, as Jesus says, "*I* will build my church, and the gates of Hades will not overcome it" (Matthew 16:18).

So as to be unmistakably clear that it is Jesus and not his followers who are the guarantors, Matthew reports directly prior to the Great Commission on how Jesus' disciples received him: "but some doubted" (Matthew 28:17). Doubters could not guarantee the success of the mission.

The Revelation of John repeatedly announces that people of all languages and cultures will belong to an innumerable throng of those who have been redeemed: "And they sang a new song: 'You are worthy to take the scroll and to open its seals, because you were slain, and with your blood you purchased men for God from every tribe and language and people and nation. You have made them to be a kingdom and priests to serve our God'" (Revelation 5:9–10; similarly Revelation 7:9; 10:11; 11:9; 13:7; 14:6; 17:15). This promise in the book of Revelation develops and fulfills a line of promises found both the Old Testament book of Daniel and also in the parables of Jesus. (See Thesis 17.)

17. Growth is included in the nature of God's kingdom, as in particular the book of Daniel makes clear in his prophetic pictures and Jesus makes clear in several parables.

Nebuchadnezzar's dream ends with a stone destroying a statue that represents the kingdoms of the world (Daniel 2:34–35), even becoming a "huge mountain" that "filled the whole earth" (Daniel 2:35; see also v. 45). Daniel comments: "In the time of those kings, the God of heaven will set up a kingdom that will never be destroyed, nor will it be left to another people. It will crush all those kingdoms and bring them to an end, but it will itself endure forever" (Daniel 2:44). Similarly, Daniel sees the end of the worldly kingdoms as represented by beasts (7:9–14, 26–27). The end of these kingdoms will come when the Son of man (Daniel 7:13)—a designation that Jesus later uses for himself—ascends into heaven and there (with the ascension) receives authority, glory, and sovereign power, with the result that "all peoples, nations and men of every language worshiped him" (Daniel 7:14). This kingdom will be everlasting (Daniel 7:14, 27). Whereas great political kingdoms will build up earthly power but then crumble at some point, the Kingdom of God will always persist, grow, and include all peoples.

Jesus actually established his kingdom at the time of the Romans—beginning with his disciples and the first churches—and foretold in many parables that it would grow until it fills the entire earth (e.g., the Parable of the Weeds: Matthew 13:24–30, 36–43; the Parable of the Mustard Seed: Matthew 13:31–32; the Parable of the Yeast: Matthew 13:33–35).

18. The promise of growth in the Old and New Testaments relates to all levels: the internal as well as the external, the spiritual and the material, the individual and the corporate or communal, etc.

The internal and external growth of the kingdom of God and of the church of Jesus Christ does not automatically mean that every individual Christian church, denomination, or group participates in this growth. God can indeed chasten his church or allow apostate churches to completely die out (see Revelation 2:5; Romans 11:20–21). Old Testament Israel always found means to continue, often with only a "stump" out of which new branches grew; however, large parts of Israel were judged. In the same way, the church of Jesus has a guarantee of existence, but this guarantee does not apply to every component part of Christianity.

The growth that is promised is no reason to feel Christian superiority, for God grants the growth *despite* (not because of) our participation. Paul also admonishes us, "So, if you think you are standing firm, be careful that you don't fall!" (1 Corinthians 10:12).

19. The histories of salvation and mission belong inseparably together, and for this reason our future, prophesied hope (eschatology) is integral to world mission.

The history of salvation is rooted in the Triune God. This history unfolds in a triple set of stages, running from creation through the fall of mankind toward the grand goal of eternal fellowship with God in a new heaven and a new earth, beginning with the return of Jesus. Then the entire creation will live in peace ("shalom"), harmony, and justice under the lordship of Christ (Ephesians 1:10; Colossians 1:20). For that reason, the history of creation, humanity, and God's mission is to be understood as simply linear and teleological, not cyclical. This truth already applies in the Old Testament and especially with regard to God's covenant with Abraham (Genesis 12:1–3), which was designed for the blessing of all peoples and for the coming of the Messiah.

In his ministry, Jesus seized upon prophetic and apocalyptic elements of Old Testament eschatology, both to fulfill them and to expand them into a still greater future vision. This fulfilled and expanded eschatology encompasses the creation, the proclamation that the kingdom of God is near in Jesus, and the future moment when the kingdom of God will comprise the entire world, because all peoples will have heard the gospel and Jesus will come again (Matthew 24:14; 26:13; 28:19; Mark 13:10; 14:9). Ultimately, it encompasses the eternal kingdom of God in which believers will sit together along with Abraham, with all the believers throughout history, and with Jesus himself. According to Matthew, the Great Commission clearly demonstrates its eschatological dimension under the Lordship of Jesus.

For that reason, Paul and the other apostles linked the eschatology realized in Christ (most clearly recognized in the resurrection, as indicated in Ephesians 1:18–21) with the proclamation of the realized kingdom of God, in which God will make all his promises and prophecies true. World mission is the time between Pentecost and the return of Christ; it is framed by fulfilled and unfulfilled eschatology. In the final event, it even goes beyond humanity to comprise the entire "creation" (Romans 8:20; see 8:17–25).

20. To become a follower of Jesus means to escape judgment here and in eternity and to personally experience the power of the resurrection.

For this reason, a personal hope for the future and the individual's eschatology, as well as a future hope and eschatology of the entirety of humankind and, indeed, the entire creation, is at the center of the gospel.

In addition to individual eschatology, general eschatology is also closely linked with the history of salvation and the gospel (Romans 8:17–25). Here I am limiting myself to the areas of eschatology that, according to early confessions of faith, are binding for all Christian churches and are common to all. For instance, it is said regarding Jesus in the Apostles' Creed that "he will come again to judge the living and the dead." The creed closes with the words, "I believe in ... the resurrection of the body and the life everlasting." The glorious return of Christ, the judgment, and the final resurrection mark the end of world mission and the beginning of eternal life, to which world mission alludes and toward which it aims.

21. World mission speaks of both judgment and grace, death and resurrection, warning and joyful anticipation, and it does not allow itself to be taken in with one-sided optimism or pessimism.

In one of his parables regarding the growth of the kingdom of God, the Parable of the Weeds (Matthew 13:24–30, 36–43), Jesus states clearly that not only the kingdom of God but also evil will prosper and mature. Evil may mature only because God also allows his church to grow and mature. Were the church of Jesus not in the world, the final judgment would have come upon the earth long ago (cf. Genesis 18:22–23).

Wherever the church and the world become too optimistic, we must soberly proclaim that this world is fallen, humankind is evil, and the world can be saved only through hope in Christ. Wherever the church and the world become too pessimistic, the great hope for the future must be proclaimed, which casts a shadow over the here-and-now and gives us a taste of things to come.

In situations ripe for judgment, Christians should not spread panic, resignation, and an end-times attitude. Rather, Christians should pray and act for their people as Abraham did (Genesis 18:20–33) and not behave like Jonah (Jonah 4:1–5) or Jesus' disciples (Luke 9:54–55), who desired judgment and doom. They should resemble Abraham, Moses, and the many prophets who have stood in the gap for the church and the world (Psalm 106:23; Ezekiel 22:30, cf. 13:5). In such situations ripe for judgment, the church must first be self-critical, repent, and change directions, above all because doing so can also lead to a change of direction in a society or societies: "If my people, who are called by my name, will humble themselves and pray and seek my face and turn from their wicked ways, then will I hear from heaven and will forgive their sin and will heal their land" (2 Chronicles 7:14).

When everything seems catastrophic for believers, perhaps because of severe persecution and martyrdom, believers should seek to also celebrate the grace already received, the resurrection, and our hope for the life to come.

22. The growth and the final success of the kingdom of God do not exclude the suffering of Jesus' Church. Rather, it encompasses suffering.

Paul did not become arrogant or unrealistic as a result of knowing the peace with God that is achieved by Jesus' grace. Rather, he wrote, "Not only so, but we also rejoice in our sufferings, because we know that suffering produces perseverance; perseverance, character; and character, hope. And hope does not disappoint us, because God has poured out his love into our hearts by the Holy Spirit, whom he has given us" (Romans 5:3–5).

23. World mission is accompanied by martyrdom. Christian suffering is a continuation of Christ's suffering and receives its distinctiveness from this.

The church's suffering cannot be understood unless one looks at Calvary. Martyrdom belongs to the nature of the church, although it is never voluntarily sought. Suffering is an integral feature of the church and its mission: "We must go through many hardships to enter the kingdom of God" (Acts 14:22). For that reason, Paul wrote, "In fact, everyone who wants to live a godly life in Christ Jesus will be persecuted" (2 Timothy 3:12). And from the Old Testament Paul draws the following teaching: "At that time the son born in the ordinary way persecuted the son born by the power of the Spirit. It is the same now" (Galatians 4:29). Every Old Testament prophet was persecuted (Acts 7:51–53; 1 Thessalonians 2:14–15; Hebrews 11:35–38; 12:1). Indeed, Jesus himself announced to his disciples, "If they persecuted me, they will persecute you also" (John 15:20).

24. Persecution does not automatically lead to church growth or to purification and strengthening of the faith.

Persecution can lead to a strengthening of the church, as has occurred recently in China. However, it can also weaken the Jesus' church, for instance in the prior German Democratic Republic. Persecution can also even completely extinguish the church, as has repeatedly happened throughout history on a regional basis, such as in areas of the Near East. Even if martyrdom should sometimes lead to abundant fruit, there is no automatic relationship between the two. Rather, it is a matter of the grace of God.

According to the Parable of the Sower (Matthew 13:3–8, 20–22), persecution of and pressure upon the faith are as dangerous as wealth and greed. Which is a greater threat for the faith, persecution or wealth? Christians in the West have tended to glorify Christian persecution, and Christians in countries where they experience persecution have tended to glorify freedom and affluence. The success of mission and evangelization cannot be forced or automatically expected, either through great freedom or through persecution.

25. Christianity is not a fair-weather religion whose followers encounter no problems and know nothing about difficulties.

The dubious nature of all teachings promising that a truly believing Christian will experience only wealth, health, or other blessings is clear from Romans 5:1–5. I emphasize the word *only* here, because God can and will give all these things to those (Matthew 6:25–34) who keep his commands and serve the cause of peace within the creation, but at the time that he considers appropriate.

Christian fair-weather prophets cut believers off from the invaluable experience of a significant implication and application of their faith, namely patience, testing, and hope, three things that even the Lord Jesus Christ, our role model, had to learn (Hebrews 5:8).

SECTION II: THE ENTIRETY OF THE HOLY SCRIPTURES JUSTIFIES WORLD MISSION

26. In the New Testament, world mission is not primarily justified by Jesus' Great Commission but rather by the Old Testament.

If one looks at the New Testament passages on the justification of mission efforts, it is astonishing to observe that at those points where Jesus or specifically Jesus' Great Commission is quoted, the Old Testament is almost always quoted as well. The Great Commission is the fulfillment of the Old Testament. In a certain sense, it was the completion of that which had long been foreseen, prepared for, and partially fulfilled but was now finally to be placed into high gear.

The letter to the Romans provides an obvious example. In this letter, Paul continuously quotes from the Old Testament (e.g., Habakkuk 2:4) to justify mission. In Romans 15:14, he seamlessly segues from Old Testament quotations about the peoples of the world and goes directly to his practical mission plans, repeating much of what he had already said in the introduction. If one contrasts the introduction (Romans 1:1–15) with the concluding section of Romans (15:14–16:27), one recognizes mission as the current occasion for the letter and in the process finds the topic of the letter in the first and last verses (Romans 1:1–6; 16:25–27). "Obedience to the faith" is to be proclaimed and planted among all peoples, as the Old Testament had stated in advance (compare, for example, Romans 15:21 with Isaiah 52:15 and the broader context of Isaiah 52:5–15, from which Paul often quotes in Romans).

Acts 13:46–49 reports that Paul and Barnabas were rejected by the Jews and explains why they turned to the Gentiles in Antioch. In this connection, they quote Isaiah 49:6 (= Acts 13:47): "For this is what the Lord commanded us: 'I have made you a light for the Gentiles, that you may bring salvation to the ends of the earth.' " The context of the passage in Isaiah makes it clear that the apostles are taking up a Great Commission proclaimed already in the Old Testament: "It is too small a thing for you

to be my servant to restore the tribes of Jacob and bring back those of Israel I have kept. I will also make you a light for the Gentiles, that you may
bring my salvation to the ends of the earth" (Isaiah 49:6).

In his final address to the Apostolic Council in Acts 15:13–21, James justifies Paul's right to proclaim the gospel to Gentiles by using Amos 9:11–12
(see also Isaiah 61:4; Psalm 22:27–28; Zechariah 8:22). There, the rebuild-
ing of "David's fallen tent" (for James, the church), the remnant of the
Jews, is brought together with those Gentiles who come in ("many peoples and the inhabitants of many cities"). As a justification for preaching
the gospel to the Gentile Cornelius, Peter links Jesus' Great Commission
to the Old Testament: "He commanded us to preach to the people and to
testify that he is the one whom God appointed as judge of the living and
the dead. All the prophets testify about him that everyone who believes
in him receives forgiveness of sins through his name" (Acts 10:42–43).

27. The Old Testament rationale for New Testament mis-
sion shows that world mission is a direct continuation of
God's actions of salvation history since the Fall of man and
the choosing of Abraham.

In the Great Commission according to Luke, Jesus expressly confirmed
the Old Testament's justification of New Testament mission: " 'This is
what I told you while I was still with you: Everything must be fulfilled
that is written about me in the Law of Moses, the Prophets and the
Psalms.' Then he opened their minds so they could understand the Scriptures. He told them, 'This is what is written: The Christ will suffer and
rise from the dead on the third day, and repentance and forgiveness of
sins will be preached in his name to all nations, beginning at Jerusalem.
You are witnesses of these things' " (Luke 24:43–48).

These words from Jesus do not simply indicate that his coming, the cross,
and the resurrection were described in all the several parts of the Old
Testament. Rather, world mission is also directly mentioned, in that forgiveness would be proclaimed to all nations.

28. The choosing of the Old Testament people of the cove-nant occurred with regard to reaching all peoples, such that world mission is already a topic found in the Old Testament.

Abraham, Isaac, and Jacob were called so that all peoples of the earth could be blessed (Genesis 12:3; 18:18; 22:17; 26:4; 28:14). Jonah was wrong when he desired salvation exclusively for the Jews and envisioned only judgment for heathen peoples (Jonah 4:1–3).

The promise to the patriarchs is repeatedly cited as the reason for mission efforts among non-Jews (Luke 1:54–55, 72; Acts 3:25–26; Romans 4:13–25; Ephesians 3:3–4; Galatians 3:7–9, 14; Hebrews 6:13–20; 11:12).

29. For this reason, in the Old Testament there are already many examples of Gentiles hearing the message of God through the Jews and finding faith in the one true God. Moreover, many passages from the Old Testament prophets are directed at Gentile peoples.

The book of Ruth reports on the conversion of a Gentile, and the book of Jonah reports that Jonah went on a missionary journey to Nineveh, despite his initial desire to avoid making the trip. As a result, Nineveh was converted. Virtually all the Old Testament prophets called upon Gentile peoples to repent. Naaman the Syrian, Moses' father-in-law, and the prostitute Rahab are only three of many examples of people who were born Gentiles but turned to the living God. Circulars by world rulers directed at all peoples, in which they praise the God of Israel, are frequently found in the Old Testament (including the books of Daniel, Esther, Ezra, and Nehemiah).

30. Accordingly, world mission efforts cannot be presented and practiced independently of the Old Testament, the history of salvation in the Old Testament, and the destiny of the Jewish people.

Paul documents this truth above all in Romans 9–11. In the process, two sides have to be considered regarding the relationship of Christian mission to the Jewish people: the election of the Jews, on one hand, and their prevailing disobedience on the other hand. "As far as the gospel is concerned, they are enemies on your account; but as far as election is concerned, they are loved on account of the patriarchs" (Romans 11:28). Paul also makes it clear that the future turning of the people of Israel to their Messiah Jesus Christ will have unimagined positive effects on the evangelization of all peoples (Romans 11:15, 24–26).

31. The letter to the Romans also demonstrates that world mission has to rest upon healthy biblical teaching and that a healthy systematic theology always leads to mission.

The letter to the Romans is written from the standpoint of practical mission work and seeks to establish a foundation for the legitimacy and necessity of global proclamation of the gospel. The letter to the Romans is at the same time a systematic biblical presentation of the gospel and of the Christian faith. It depicts Paul as a missionary with a deeply moved heart and soul as well as a highly educated theologian whom God used to formulate significant portions of the New Testament.

In the letter to the Romans, Paul wishes to proclaim the gospel to all people without exception, regardless of their language, culture, race/ethnicity ("Greeks and non-Greeks," Romans 1:14), education, or social class ("both the wise and the foolish," Romans 1:14). It is for that reason that he wishes to come to Rome (Romans 1:15). From this practical missionary concern, Paul directly transitions to the primary topic. In Romans 1:16–17, Paul begins his instruction with "For ... ." In the end, Paul returns to his practical missionary concerns. Paul thus substantiates by way of instruction in Romans 1:16–15:13 what he wants to do practically according to Romans 1:8–15 and 15:14–16:27. The "obedience of faith" has to be comprehensively presented and proclaimed and planted in all peoples.

Whoever only conducts missions practically and thinks that he can thereby dispense with doctrine ends up conducting mission only on his own behalf and disregarding why God has said what he has given us in the Scriptures.

SECTION III: MISSION IN LIGHT OF CULTURAL DIVERSITY

32. The diversity of peoples and cultures is principally not a consequence of sin but rather desired by God. What is to be discarded from a culture is only that which expressly contradicts God's holy will, and not the diversity of human expression and lifestyle.

God is the Creator of all peoples: "From one man he made every nation of men, that they should inhabit the whole earth: and he determined the times for them and the exact places where they should live" (Acts 17:26; cf. Deuteronomy 32:7–9; Psalm 74:17; 86:9). For that reason, a Christian must love people from all cultures and respect the otherness of other cultures (Revelation 1:6–8; Psalm 66:8).

The variety of distinct cultures and languages is not to be understood negatively as a consequence of sin. To get an appropriate perspective on the multiplicity of cultures around the world, one should look carefully at what God did through the confusion of languages at the building of the Tower of Babel (Genesis 11:1–9), and especially notice how this relates to the teaching of the previous parts of the book of Genesis. The sin to which God responded at Babel was not only arrogance, seen in the people's desire "that we may make a name for ourselves"; in their sin they also desired a city with a large tower, "otherwise we will be scattered over the face of the whole earth." They were resisting God's plan that people actively begin inhabiting the entire planet. Through the confusion of languages, God restrained their arrogance but also restored humanity to the destiny and mandate, indeed even the command that he had given humankind, which was to spread throughout the entire earth ("fill the earth," Genesis 1:28; 9:1). He envisioned the splitting up of humanity into a diversity of families, peoples, and cultures as well as professions, abilities, and services. As we understand the book of Genesis, it is a positive development that from the sons of Noah "came the people who were scattered over the earth" (Genesis 9:19) and that "the maritime peoples spread out into their territories by their clans within their nations, each with its own language" (Genesis 10:5). For this reason, the emergence of individual peoples can be explained through family trees (Genesis 10:1–32), at the end of which one reads: "From these the nations spread out over the earth after the flood." Up to the present day, cultures and languages continuously change with each new generation, and in fact new cultures gradually develop in the process.

God repeatedly announced in the Old Testament that he envisioned the salvation of all peoples (e.g., Genesis 12:3; Isaiah 49:6) in such a manner that does not indicate that the existence of multiple people groups and cultures is a problem. Their problem is the lack of salvation. Jonah's Great Commission illustrates God's intent that salvation be proclaimed to all peoples already in Old Testament times. Pentecost makes it clear that Jesus' church transcends all cultural and language barriers. The church is for that reason inherently multicultural (Revelation 5:9–10; 7:9; 10:11; 11:9; 13:7; 14:6; 17:15; Daniel 7:13–14; Ephesians 2:11–19).

33. Christians have been freed from all sorts of cultural bondage. They no longer have to recognize human traditions and commands in addition to God's commands.

This becomes particularly clear in Mark 7:1–13, where Jesus vehemently criticized the Pharisees because they raised their human culture to the level of God's obligatory commands. "You have a fine way of setting aside the commands of God in order to observe your own traditions!" (Mark 7:9). We are always in danger of wrongly absolutizing our own traditions (even our religious traditions) and making them the standard by which other cultures are measured. In so doing, we place ourselves in the position of God, who alone is the lawgiver (James 4:12) and who alone has the right to set standards by which all cultures are to be measured.

34. Christians can judge other cultures in light of the Bible when and if they have learned to distinguish between their own cultures, even their own devout culture, and the commands of God that are valid for all cultures.

Mark 7:1–13 is again the best starting point. Very honorable, pious motives initially prompted the Pharisees to issue numerous guidelines in addition to the word of God—and even against God's word—and to make them binding for everyone. Jesus criticized them because they had made themselves into lawgivers alongside God: "They worship me in vain; their teachings are but rules taught by men" (Mark 7:7; Matthew 15:9).

Beyond the truth claims that undergird Christian mission, there should be no claim to superiority on the part of one's own culture above another culture. There should also be no claim to superiority of one's own religious culture or expression of Christianity. Unfortunately, due to political and national issues, there have been times when Christians have exported their cultures, what Jesus described as "rules taught by men," along with the gospel. At this point, Christians should also make a clear distinction between the church and state, recognizing that knowledge of the truths of Jesus does not make one infallible in questions of culture and politics. Indeed, Christians are citizens living among other citizens, just like everyone else. Colonialism and racism must be kept separate from Christian proclamation.

35. No religion contains such self-criticism in its fundamental writings as Old Testament Judaism and New Testament Christianity.

Jesus rejects the words of the Pharisees, "God, I thank you that I am not like other men," and praises the words of the tax collector, "God have mercy on me, a sinner" (Luke 18:11–14). Faith begins in the Bible with the recognition of one's own inadequacy. Christians cannot back away from this reality, even when discussing questions of ultimate truth.

There is no other religion in which the faith's adherents are depicted in such a bad light as in the Jewish and Christian Scriptures. The mistakes of their most important leaders are laid unsparingly bare; for example, Moses, David, and Paul were all murderers; and Peter committed the worst: the betrayal of Jesus. God had to use a rooster to bring Peter to his senses!

The fact that Jews and Christians are sinners and capable of evil is vividly clear in the Bible. Most of the time, the primary focus is not on the atrocities and errors of heathen peoples but on the apparent or actual people of God. The Bible does not recognize belief and unbelief according to racial, ethnic, or national membership. Gentiles and unbelieving Jews are for that reason labeled with the same words in the Old Testament as well as in the New Testament.

Christianity itself becomes an abhorrent religion if it renounces the true power of faith (2 Timothy 3:5: "having a form of godliness but denying its power") or when it places human laws and commands in the place of divine revelation (Mark 7:1–13; Isaiah 28:13–14). For instance, Jews are criticized because they overlook that which is essential, namely Jesus (John 5:39), and because they strive toward God but do not actually live in a suitable manner (Romans 2).

36. To show regard for an individual in the church on the basis of cultural, economic, educational, ethnic, racial, or other points of view contradicts the nature of God and of the Christian faith.

God does not show favoritism. Not only are state courts instructed not to show partiality (Deuteronomy 1:17; 10:17–18; 16:18–20; 2 Chronicles 19:7; Proverbs 18:5; 24:23; Job 13:10; Isaiah 3:9), but New Testament churches are also to reject any favoritism (Colossians 3:25; Ephesians 6:9). James writes: "My brothers, as believers in our glorious Lord Jesus Christ, don't show favoritism. ... If you really keep the royal law found in Scripture, 'Love your neighbor as yourself,' you are doing right. But if you show favoritism, you sin and are convicted by the law as lawbreakers. ... Speak and act as those who are going to be judged by the law that gives freedom" (James 2:1–12).

For this reason, every form of racism must be foreign to the New Testament church. Humanity is a single race and family in which all individuals, peoples, and ethnic groups are equal and equally worthy. Jesus died for all people, and people from all cultures and languages will praise him in heaven for eternity (Revelation 4:11; 21:1).

37. Christians are citizens of the world!

At all times, Christians should properly have the entire world in view. They should never have only their own family, their own people, or their own country in view. They do not believe in a tribal god, but rather in the Creator who has made the entire world and all peoples and wants all to be redeemed (Genesis 1:1; John 3:16; Matthew 28:18-20; Revelation 4:11; 21:1). They also do not belong to an international club with narrow-minded concerns. Rather, they belong to Jesus' international church, which is not bound by language, people, culture, social class, age, gender, or any other factor that separates people (Romans 1:14; Ephesians 1:13–14; Revelation 5:9–10; Revelation 21:24–25). And they belong to the church, whose mandate could not be greater and more international: "Therefore go and make disciples of all nations" (Matthew 28:19).

Indeed, Christians want every individual soul as well as the entire world to be saved, and this desire should be expressed visibly as well as invisibly! Their perspective is private when they are praying, but it is also very public. It has to do with the individual's relationship to God and with the entire world's relationship to God. It also affects our relationship with our immediate neighbor and our relationship with all fellow human beings.

Christian hope is hope for all cultures and nations: "In his name the nations will put their hope" (Matthew 12:21; similarly Romans 15:12). God does not show partiality; "For this we labor and strive, that we have put our hope in the living God, who is the Savior of all men, and especially of those who believe" (1 Timothy 4:10).

38. Since Christians belong solely to Christ and are solely under the restraint of his word, they not only see their own

and other cultures critically but are obligated, out of love, to adapt to the culture of others.

In 1 Corinthians 9:19–23, Paul justifies the necessity of adapting to others in evangelization: "Though I am free and belong to no man, I make myself a slave to everyone, to win as many as possible. To the Jews I became like a Jew, to win the Jews. To those under the law I became like one under the law (though I myself am not under the law), so as to win those under the law. To those not having the law I became like one not having the law (though I am not free from God's law but am under Christ's law), so as to win those not having the law. To the weak I became weak, to win the weak. I have become all things to all men so that by all possible means I might save some. I do all this for the sake of the gospel that I may share in its blessings."

Luther poignantly generalized and summarized this complementarity: "A Christian man is the most free lord of all, and subject to none; a Christian man is the most dutiful servant of all, and subject to every one."

39. Christians are responsible not only for declaring the message of redemption in Jesus Christ but also for ensuring that it is understood.

A Christian accustomed to his own culture may not notice that in the best case he is not understood and in the worst case he could actually hinder (cf. 1 Corinthians 9:12) an understanding of the gospel due to his cultural baggage.

The fact that the words of Jesus Christ and the gospel about his work on earth were not disseminated in Aramaic (or Hebrew) as part of the Bible but rather in a Greek translation or via Greek authorship establishes that it was intended to reach people in a language that was as widely understandable as possible.

Additionally, the gospel of Jesus Christ was not announced simply in one document. Rather, the one gospel is found in four recorded versions (Matthew, Mark, Luke, and John) aimed at four different target groups.

This rationale also establishes that the Bible should be translated into every language and that the gospel can and should be expressed in every dialect and every cultural form.

40. World mission does not bypass preexisting sociological facts; rather, its strategy is determined by those facts. For that reason, Paul founded churches in areas with a high population density, left it to those churches to penetrate their surrounding regions, and went on to found new churches in areas unreached by the gospel.

Paul primarily founded churches in centrally located cities, quickly installed elders whom he had trained, and traveled on. The complete evangelistic penetration of a region with the gospel was left to the city church. For example, we read the following about the church in Thessalonica: "And so you became a model to all the believers in Macedonia and Achaia. The Lord's message rang out from you not only in Macedonia and Achaia—your faith in God has become known everywhere. Therefore we do not need to say anything about it" (1 Thessalonians 1:7-8).

When Paul wrote in Romans 15:19 that "from Jerusalem all the way around to Illyricum, I have fully proclaimed the gospel of Christ," he did not mean that he proclaimed the gospel to every single individual there. Rather, he meant that he had founded churches in all the important areas. The same meaning pertains to his statement that "now that there is no more place for me to work in these regions" (Romans 15:23). Paul was moving on to look for areas with people "who have not heard" (Romans 15:20), where preaching had not occurred (Romans 15:21), and where no indigenous churches existed.

41. Not only is the proclamation of the gospel to be formulated for various cultures, but the gospel should be enculturated in the life of each community and its entire culture.

Just as God spoke through prophets in the people's language, and just as Christ became a human being in space and time whom people could see and understand—in the process linking the word of God to the history and culture of all peoples—so it is God's desire that the gospel today should not only reach people from all cultures but penetrate them and demonstrate through their new expressions that the gospel is not bound to any certain space or time, let alone to any respective preacher.

Since God himself has brought about the diversity of cultures (Thesis 32), he does not want to limit this diversity through the gospel. Rather, he wants to strengthen and refine it. It is not a coincidence that through world mission—above all through the work of Bible translation—many small cultures and languages of the world have been retained.

Let us consider a parallel to our individuality. Does God destroy our personality when we become believers? Does he make everyone the same? If that were the case, something would be terribly wrong. After all, God created us with distinctive personalities, and he loves the tremendous diversity which he has created in humanity. God does not employ coercion, so that in redemption he forces us to become something truly other than what he created us to be. This was the point of wisdom in older theological slogans about redemption renewing creation or about grace restoring nature. Therefore, coercion and compulsion are the marks of evil, indeed of the devil (e.g., Mark 5:25). Evil and the devil do not support or help us to become our true selves; rather, they mislead and coerce us and bring us to the point of sinning before we manage to reflect on things. The devil is the enemy of self-control, of deliberation on what is truly good for us and whence the power comes to implement it.

In contrast, God gives us everything, and he wants the distinctive personalities he has created to demonstrate self-control and act calmly and with a level head so that God will then move within us with the power of the Holy Spirit. To become a Christian does not mean to lose one's personality. Rather, it means to gain one's personality, freed from evil ballast. When God's Spirit works in and through individuals, it makes them into true personalities and not into marionettes. As a clear illustration of this fact, various gifts of the Spirit are granted to every Christian so that everyone can serve the same purpose, but each in his own particular way (Romans 12:4–7; 1 Peter 4:12–13; 1 Corinthians 12; Ephesians 4:11–13).

Something similar applies to cultures. God does not destroy them; rather, God's Spirit frees them from evil and leads them to greater blossoming. In the end, a divine diversity of cultures is erected, as seen in the church of Jesus Christ around the world, not a uniform church or a uniform culture.

SECTION IV: MISSION AND RELIGIOUS FREEDOM—TWO SIDES OF THE SAME COIN

42. Dialogue, in the sense of peaceful contention, honest and patient listening, self-critical reflection, winsome and modest presentation of one's own point of view, and learning from others, is a Christian virtue.

A dialogue between convinced Christians and adherents of other religions and worldviews is possible in the sense that Christians should willingly speak with others peacefully about their faith (1 Peter 3:15–16: "Be prepared to give an answer ... But do this with gentleness and respect"), willingly listen to others (James 1:19), learn from the life experiences of others in many areas (see the entire book of Proverbs), and remain open to having their own lives and behavior questioned.

43. Dialogue in the sense of giving up Christian truth claims or giving up world mission is inconceivable without abandoning Christianity.

If one interprets dialogue to mean suspending the innermost truth claims of Jesus Christ (John 14:6), of the gospel (Romans 1:16–17; 2:16), and of the word of God (2 Timothy 3:16–17; Hebrews 4:12–13; John 17:17), or as suspending the missional essence of the Christian faith (either temporarily or in principle) and placing biblical revelation on a par with the revelations of other religions (either fully or in part), then dialogue cannot be reconciled with Christian mission or with the essence of Christianity.

The truth claim of the Christian faith is expressed above all in its teaching on the final judgment and on eternal life. Hebrews 6:1–2 speaks of "the resurrection of the dead and eternal judgment" as two of the six most important foundations of the faith. The church has held to these truths throughout all times, as demonstrated by its confession of faith: "he will come to judge the living and the dead."

However, that conviction also implies that we Christians must leave judgment up to God and do not know his judgment in advance. Christians are glad that God himself is the judge and that every final judgment is withheld. Only God himself can look into the heart of an individual, and in the end we do not know his judgment: "Man looks at the outward appearance, but the Lord looks at the heart" (1 Samuel 17:7).

44. Paul's address in Athens shows how good and important it is to study other religions and worldviews, including their texts, and to adjust the terminology and starting point of our proclamation so as to address the adherents of other religions and worldviews intellectually and linguistically.

According to the book of Acts, the apostles engaged the mission discussion precisely at those points where the Christian worldview and listeners' worldviews diverged, while simultaneously developing whatever common presuppositions were to be found. For that reason, when they spoke with Jews, they did not discuss the creation and the inspiration of the Old Testament. Rather, they entered directly into discussion about Jesus Christ and placed their presentation of Christ into the unfolding story of God's redemptive work since the earliest times in the Old Testament. With the Gentiles, they went significantly further back and also discussed creation, explaining what could be known and was presupposed about the Creator in the respective culture and then presented the biblical testimony (e.g., Acts 14:8–18; 17:16–34). For this reason, Paul was able to attest to an awareness of the existence of the Creator by reference to quotations from Greek philosophers in his famous speech in the Areopagus in Athens (Acts 17:16–34) without expressly reverting to the biblical testimony.

This address demonstrates that Paul had studied the Greek philosophers intensively and had specifically planned his address for this particular audience. He also did not simply revert to generally known dictums. Rather, he also relied on obscure texts. This strategy is illustrated by the fact that in Titus 1:12 Paul quoted Epimenides, whom he also cited in Acts 17:28. Paul understood the philosophers and paraphrased their thoughts, for instance in pointing out that God does not need any help from people (Acts 17:25). That thought did indeed contradict Greek religious practice but could be found almost word for word in Plato, Euripides, and other Greek philosophers.

Paul's address thus becomes the classic example of a missions sermon. It has a lot to say to a missionary today, not only with regard to content but also in terms of the manner by which one should proceed. In Acts 14:15–17, Paul proceeded very similarly with respect to the worshipers of Zeus, even though we do not come across quotations from philosophers at that point—perhaps because of the less educated audience or simply due to the brief form of reporting. Many commentators have pointed out that the address in Acts 17 is only a practical application of the first chapters of the letter to the Romans (especially Romans 1:17–2:4).

45. Ethics and mission belong together. Christian witness is not an ethics-free space; it requires an ethical foundation so that we truly do what Christ has instructed us to do.

In 1 Peter 3:15–17, one finds an instance of complementarity. On one hand, we learn of the necessity of Christian testimony, indeed apologetics (in the Greek text, the word *apologia* originally signified an address used to defend oneself before a court). On the other hand, we are also told to demonstrate "gentleness and respect," thus acknowledging the dignity of other human beings: "Always be prepared to give an answer to everyone who asks you to give the reason (*apologia*) for the hope that you have. But do this with gentleness and respect." The dignity of human beings does not allow us to hide our hope. Rather, we want to express it clearly, explain it, and defend it. And yet, being challenged with questions behind which evil intentions lie does not authorize us to trample our questioner's dignity underfoot. Both sides complement each other, in the same way that both are essential building blocks of our faith.

According to 1 Peter 3:15–17, people do not speak directly with God when they speak with us. On one hand, we can certainly be God's messengers and bear witness to the hope that is in us. On the other hand, we are saved solely through God's grace and not based on our own virtue. We want people to find peace with God, receive his forgiveness, and trust God as the sole truth. However, they have not sinned against us. They should not bow before us; we are not the embodiment of truth nor are we in possession of the truth in everything we say. No Christian is a "Doctor Know-It-All." Rather, Christians are normal people who have special knowledge only insofar as they bear witness to the revealed truth of Jesus Christ and the gospel as written in the Bible, and to their personal experience of it.

Whoever presumes to have found the truth in Jesus—the truth about our relationship to God and how we find peace with God through grace, forgiveness, and redemption—and invokes the written revelation of Judeo-Christian tradition must simultaneously take into consideration everything that the Scriptures teach regarding content and demeanor, which represents serious restraints on how we converse with someone who thinks differently. Truth and love (Ephesians 4:15) belong together, especially in dialogue and in missionary witness.

46. Gentleness is not only an inevitable consequence of the fact that Christians proclaim the God of love and should love our neighbor. Rather, it is also a consequence of the knowledge that Christians are themselves only pardoned sinners and are not God.

Our partner in conversation needs to be reconciled with our Creator, not with us. For that reason, we can always step back, admit our own finiteness and shortcomings, and point out clearly that we can only claim authority with regard to another person insofar as we genuinely and understandably proclaim the good news. Showing esteem for people is a consequence of the fact that we look at people with God's eyes, i.e., as his creatures, made in the image of God. That prohibits us from treating anyone as sub-human or as mentally inferior if he or she disagrees with us.

Christians do not have an answer to every question. Rather, they can only defend God's message where God has revealed himself throughout the course of history in the Scriptures and in Christ. Jesus strictly distinguished between God's commands and the commands of men within their respective religious traditions and cultures (e.g., Mark 7:1–15; see Theses 33 and 34). A Christian cannot approach interactions with the claim to know and be able to defend the truth about everything. Rather, he or she can only speak about truth claims as a fallible person at those points where God authorizes it, and these understandings are to be tested and refined repeatedly (Romans 12:2). Therefore, Christians can learn much from their discussion partners without having to lower their own sights when it comes to central questions of the faith.

47. Mission efforts esteem human rights and do not desire to disregard the dignity of human beings. Rather, mission efforts seek to honor and foster human dignity.

Christians always look at other people as in the image of God (Genesis 1:26–27; 5:1), even if those individuals have other views. From the point of view of Christianity, human rights are not derived from whether one believes in God or is a Christian. Rather, they are grounded in the fact that everyone is in equal measure created by God and according to God's image. Indeed, everyone is created equal, whether man or woman. For that reason, all people should be treated equally, without showing favoritism toward any person (Romans 2:11; James 2:9). Some religions grant human rights only to their own adherents. Christians, however, should defend the human rights of, pray for, and love their enemies (Matthew 5:44; Luke 6:27).

48. It is reprehensible to bring about conversions through the use of coercion, deceitfulness, trickery, or bribery. By definition, such actions cannot result in a true conversion and turning towards God from the depths of one's heart in belief and trust.

A conversion is (more specifically, it should be) a deeply personal, well-thought-out stirring of an individual's heart towards God. When people say to us that they want to become Christians, we always have to grant them room and time to decide, refrain from badgering them, and not hastily baptize them in an unexamined manner. Instead, we should be sure that they truly know what they are doing and are acting from a position of conviction and belief.

Honesty and transparency should also hold sway as far as what the Christian faith consists of and what is expected of Christians after their conversion. Christianity is not a secret association. Rather, it is open to the general public and transparent to everyone. Christians have nothing to hide (Matthew 10:26–27) or to conceal beforehand, only to reveal later to the initiated. Jesus said to those who wanted to become his followers, "Suppose one of you wants to build a tower. Will he not first sit down and estimate the cost to see if he has enough money to complete it?" (Luke 14:28; see verses 27–33). Christians have to help people count the cost and not cause them to make premature commitments, only to discover later that they have been misled.

49. Peaceful mission efforts have been essentially embedded as a human right.

Mission efforts have repeatedly been embedded as a human right in global human rights texts. Human rights in missions are derived from the right to freedom of expression (including freedom of the press), as well as freedom of conscience and freedom of religion. All these rights were clearly articulated in *The Universal Declaration of Human Rights*, issued by the United Nations in 1948.

On one hand, mission efforts are nothing other than an implementation of freedom of expression. Just as this freedom applies to how political parties, popular movements, advertising entities, and media outlets publish their view of things and attempt to convince others, so it also applies to religions.

Alongside this freedom is the right to public exercise of religion. This right encompasses freedom to solicit interest in one's own convictions, which may occur through the use of all sorts of media.

50. One must differentiate between advocating human rights and religious freedom for adherents of other religions, or for individuals without any religious affiliation, and endorsing their truth claims.

Though it may seem self-evident to many, yet it bears explicit mention: it is possible to advocate liberty, religious freedom, and freedom of conscience for others without implying that their convictions are true or sharing those convictions. Conversely, one never has the right to oppress another individual or group of people with whom one disagrees with regard to issues of ultimate truth.

Christians who proclaim the gospel might deeply regret with bleeding hearts that other people reject the offer of redemption in Christ, but they must never declare these people to be less than human, to attack them with words, to stir up state powers to hatred against them, to call for judgment against them, or to carry out such judgment.

Historical experience, in fact, has taught that even groups who have largely agreed on questions relating to religion have nevertheless engaged in wars against each other, even on religious issues. Many major armed conflicts have occurred within a single religious tradition, and Christianity is not an exception to this rule.

51. Religious freedom applies to all people, not only to Christians.

This is not only a political demand made upon Christians. Rather, it arises from the Christian faith itself. As already stated, God has created all people in his image (Genesis 1:26–27; 5:1), not only Christians. God desires, as the Old Testament repeatedly stresses, to be loved with all one's heart, not out of coercion. Accordingly, the innermost orientation of an individual's conscience and heart cannot be forced.

God has forbidden us from carrying out any type of sentence upon our critics or from punishing people for their unbelief. Jonah also experienced that God was more merciful toward "godless" Nineveh than was

Jonah himself, who would have preferred to have seen judgment execut-
ed against the city (Jonah 4:1–10). And Jesus clearly rejected the thinking
of his disciples, who wanted to see fire sent down from heaven upon the
villages that spurned him (Luke 9:51–56). In this light we see that Christians are forever forbidden from punishing other people for rejecting Jesus or the gospel.

**52. Since the state does not belong to any religion and is not
to proclaim the gospel but rather desires what is good and
just for all people, and because God has granted human dignity to all people since he has created everyone (Genesis
1:26–27; 5:1), Christians should work together with the adherents of all religions and worldviews for the good of society, to the extent that other groups allow this and reciprocate.**

This principle applies directly to maintaining religious freedom, to all
human rights, and fundamentally to peace and justice. Christians should
always be involved with adherents of other religions and worldviews in
seeking to establish a just state. In Romans 13:1–7, Paul did not presup-
pose that the "authorities" are Christians. On the contrary, he placed
Christians in submission to the state, which is obligated to maintain justice, regardless of which religion or worldview its representatives es-
pouse.

Paul admonished Christians, "If it is possible, as far as it depends on you,
live at peace with everyone" (Romans 12:18). In this regard, he was consistent with Jesus, who said, "Blessed are the peacemakers" (Matthew 5:9)
and "When you enter a house, first say, 'Peace to this house' " (Luke 10:5).
James, the brother of Jesus, expressed similar sentiments: "Peacemakers
who sow in peace raise a harvest of righteousness" (James 3:18). In 1
Timothy 2:1–2, Paul expanded this command to encompass the world of
politics: "I urge, then, first of all, that requests, prayers, intercession and
thanksgiving be made for everyone—for kings and all those in authority,
that we may live peaceful and quiet lives in all godliness and holiness."

Christians must build relationships of trust and love with all people, religious and non-religious. This is a precondition for peaceful and function-

ing coexistence. Tension and conflict between people can be resolved on- ly if they speak with each other.

53. The task of the state is to protect worldly justice, includ- ing religious freedom, not to promote our religion.

When we consider which tasks the New Testament ascribes to the state, we see that the propagation and promotion of a certain religion is *not* among them, but pursuing peace and justice for everyone *is* among them. Christians are subject to the state in issues of worldly justice. Indeed, Paul described the non-Christian state as nothing less than "God's servant" when it punishes Christians who do wrong (Romans 13:1–7). Despite the fact that throughout history Christians have often handled this com- pletely differently in so-called "Christian" countries, no Christian should perceive it as a compromise of the faith to advocate full religious freedom for other religions or for atheists. Rather, this understanding of religious freedom arises organically from our understanding of faith as a convic- tion of the heart and from our understanding of the biblically defined tasks of the state.

According to the biblical understanding, the state has a monopoly on the force needed to enforce justice. It has neither the task of proclaiming the gospel nor that of enlarging the Christian church, and it should keep it- self out of questions of conscience and religion (in Romans 13:1–7, Paul discusses punishment for those who *do* evil, not for how they think, which implies that the state as "God's servant" is expressly obligated to punish even Christians if they do wrong).

The state is responsible for protecting Christians only to the extent that it should protect everyone who does what is good. It should restrain or punish Christians only insofar as they impede the state's ability to pro- vide justice and peace to everyone, and it punishes everyone who plans or exercises violence, regardless of whether those actions are religiously motivated. Christians thus demand for themselves no greater right to re- ligious freedom than others. And they should want to "live at peace with everyone" (Romans 12:18), not only with those who are like them.

54. Religious freedom includes religious freedom for one's own children.

As bitter as the experience might be when the children of committed Christians do not make the Christian faith the center of their lives, and as much as the Bible calls Christians to raise children so that they will love God and their neighbors (Deuteronomy 5:6–9), raising a child also means bringing the child into adulthood, the point at which he or she becomes independent (2 Timothy 3:17; Ephesians 4:11–16). This independence includes issues of faith (2 Timothy 3:14–17; Deuteronomy 31:12–13). Exercising any form of coercion upon the next generation so that they do not leave the church is unbiblical, whether it emanates from the parents, the environment, the church, or the state. Belief in God cannot be forced. Rather, it is the most profound and most personal decision and heart attitude of each individual who turns in love toward the Creator and Redeemer who loves him or her.

The Baptists at the time of the Reformation and the later Baptist-oriented free churches expressed this understanding directly. They rejected infant baptism and accepted only the baptisms of people who demonstrated religious maturity, just as the voluntary nature of faith and of church membership was and is central for them. Since not all Evangelicals come from such churches, this view of baptism has not become universal among them. However, the need for an independent decision by young people raised in Christian homes can be clearly maintained among those who practice infant baptism, such as through the practice of confirmation, the mature Protestant view of which was devised by Martin Bucer and strongly promoted by Pietists.

In any case, the issue of not coercing one's children is common to all Evangelicals, regardless of their position on the best timing of baptism. As deeply as Evangelicals wish to guide their children to turn to Christ by example and by persuasive discussion and teaching, true conversion requires a personal decision and commitment based on an individual's own faith. Consciously Christian childrearing should seek, in reliance on the Holy Spirit, to bring young people to the point where they can make such a commitment with full understanding and without coercion (see Thesis 65).

The (international) Evangelical Alliance spoke out in favor of the most radical form of religious freedom at the time of its founding in 1846. This viewpoint recognizes a special form of religious freedom, namely that of one's own children. It excludes child rearing by the state church, denies the possibility of any culturally prescribed inheritability of the Christian faith, and rejects child rearing by coercion.

55. We need a biblically renewed point of view regarding those who violate state laws for the sake of the gospel.

Peter and the apostles evangelized despite state prohibitions (Acts 4:19–20; 5:29) and were frequently arrested and punished (e.g., Acts 12:1–3). Christians called Jesus "Lord" (Greek *kyrios*) and "king" despite state opposition ("defying Caesar's decrees," Acts 17:6–7; cf. Acts 4:12).

"We must obey God rather than men!" (Acts 5:29) does not contradict the Christian responsibility to obey those in power when they justifiably and equitably exercise their authority. However, when these authorities seek to prevent Christians from doing what God has ordered them to do or to force them to do something that God has expressly forbidden them from doing, God must take the priority. Indeed, God is the one who legitimates human authority in the first place (Romans 13:1), and his righteousness is the standard that exposes human and state injustice.

If religious freedom is suppressed and Christian mission is prohibited, Christians are justified in being peacefully disobedient.

SECTION V: CONVERSION AND SOCIAL CHANGE

56. The individual's peace with God, i.e., personal redemption owing to the gracious sacrifice of Jesus on the cross, is the first and most urgent goal of mission from which all other goals emerge.

Jesus stated very clearly in Matthew 16:26 that salvation of the soul is more important than any other matter: "What good will it be for a man if he gains the whole world, yet forfeits his soul? Or what can a man give in exchange for his soul?"

Accordingly, in his letter to the Romans, Paul first explains why both Jews and Gentiles are lost before God in their sins and why Jesus alone is the source of salvation. "Therefore, since we have been justified through faith, we have peace with God through our Lord Jesus Christ, through whom we have gained access by faith into this grace in which we now stand" (Romans 5:1–2). Beginning at this point, he speaks about personal ethics and then addresses shared, cultural, and political ethics.

57. Even if personal salvation is the first and highest goal of missions, that does not mean that there cannot be any wider objectives. Rather, all wider objectives gain their significance from personal salvation. From inner transformation follows external transformation, and from the transformation of individuals comes change in the broader, symbiotic community.

According to Matthew 28:18–20, the Great Commission contains the summons to make learners ("disciples") of all people. The first step is to address individual people so that they will change their ways; after all, baptism can be conducted only with individuals. Nevertheless, the Great Commission suggests that in this way entire "nations" are to be won over. The presence of a high percentage of Christians in a people group does not contradict the top-priority need for each individual to turn personally to God.

This personal turning to God is not the endpoint but rather the point of departure for personal renewal, and for the renewal and transformation of family, church, commerce, the state, and society. It is for this purpose that all people are to be made into disciples. When Jesus charged his disciples with the task of "teaching them to obey everything I have commanded you," he called them to convey the entire range of biblical ethics. Through this, the individual, his or her everyday life, and his or her environment will be changed and transformed, and sinful structures and visible injustices will be overcome.

58. Social work within the Christian church was institutionally anchored, from the very beginning of the New Testament church, in the office of the diaconal ministry, and this in light of cultural differences.

The installation of deacons in Acts 6 and in the New Testament church in general is of tremendous importance. It is astonishing that in the New Testament church, in addition to the offices of overseer (bishops) and elders, who are responsible for leadership and teaching, there is only one additional fixed office, namely that of deacons (Philippians 1:1; 1 Timothy 3:8–10) and deaconesses (Romans 16:1; 1 Timothy 3:11–13). Their task is of a social nature. The social responsibility of the church for its members is so institutionalized in the office of deacon and deaconess that a church without it is as unthinkable as a church without biblical teaching or leadership.

The church is socially responsible for its own members in a comprehensive manner, insofar as relatives cannot take the responsibility for providing such care upon themselves (1 Timothy 5:1–4). This does not simply entail making donations or giving symbolic assistance; rather, it is a matter of comprehensive responsibility.

59. In Acts 6, social responsibility within the church indeed has central significance, but that does not contradict the centrality of proclaiming God's word and of prayer, which was institutionalized in the offices of elder and apostle.

The apostles gave the following reason as to why they did not want to also take over the "responsibility" of caring for widows: "We will give our attention to prayer and the ministry of the word" (Acts 6:4). Prayer and proclamation of the word are slotted ahead of social engagement and provide the justification and motivation for social engagement. Ministry of the word and prayer, then, always belong together. According to 1 Samuel 12:23, the prophet Samuel's service was to pray and to teach.

Social responsibility and the social work of the diaconate may not supplant proclamation and worship services. Rather, these activities should arise organically from verbal proclamation and worship.

60. Social responsibility on the part of Christians does not stop at the boundaries of the church.

Proverbs 3:27 states clearly, "Do not withhold good from those who deserve it, when it is in your power to act." Thus, the responsibility mentioned in Galatians 6:10 certainly applies to all people, even though the "family of believers" is specifically highlighted there: "Therefore, as we have opportunity, let us do good to all people, especially to those who belong to the family of believers." We should recall that in New Testament times, people who became Christians were often oppressed and persecuted and lost their traditional forms of social support.

Since Christians should always be expressing love for their enemies, and since they are to bless those who curse them (Romans 12:14), Christians are always to help others willingly and without favoritism anywhere in the world, wherever it is possible for them do so. This includes being prepared to help individuals in emergency situations, exposing sinful social structures on the basis of biblical commands, and seeking to change such structures, albeit without violence.

For instance, this universal application of the call to love others applies when we seek to fulfill the many biblical commands to take care of widows and orphans (e.g., Deuteronomy 14:29; 16:11; 24:19–21; 25:12–13). "Religion that God our Father accepts as pure and faultless is this: to look after orphans and widows in their distress and to keep oneself from being polluted by the world" (James 1:27).

Christian hope is also hope for the poor, the weak, and the suffering, "so that the poor have hope" (Job 5:16) and "the hope of the afflicted [will never] perish" (Psalm 9:19). Those who are imprisoned unjustly are "prisoners of hope" (Zechariah 9:12); the lonely widow "puts her hope in God and continues night and day to pray and to ask God for help" (1 Timothy 5:5). This hope is for eternal fellowship with God as well as hope for change in the here-and-now.

Church history has been deeply marked by Christian movements that have powerfully demonstrated hope for all levels of society. Examples have included the Evangelical anti-slavery movement, Methodism, the Salvation Army, the Blue Cross, and deaconess associations and orders. We should seek to connect such endeavors with contemporary global development issues and, like Jesus, to demonstrate hope for every individual in the world, regardless of whether that individual has been written off by a host of others.

61. The Bible is not a book purely for private edification. On the contrary, it repeatedly addresses many social concerns.

The Bible addresses innumerable questions of familial, economic, legal, civil, and organizational importance. It speaks about inheritances, education, caring for the poor, debt, inflation, salaries, taxes, prostitution, kidnapping, property borders, compensation, judges, kings, bribery, military spending, self-defense, caring for creation, perjury, abortion, profits, the welfare of the aged, protection of the blind and the deaf, and much more. Indeed, most sins mentioned expressly in the New Testament are social sins. Therefore, any attempts to understand the Bible and the law of God as consisting simply of instructions for individuals are to be rejected. It is naturally the case that all Christian ethics and every change within the individual and in everyday life begin with the individual, but they have immense social consequences.

The Bible is so permeated by ordinances and instruction relevant to our communal and social existence that any attempt to distill the biblical law found in the Old and New Testaments down to something exclusively applicable to the private sphere of life is equivalent to abolishing the law and its goal, which is a just peace (*shalom*).

62. Whoever is in favor of diaconal work must also address the reasons why certain emergencies exist in the first place, as the Old Testament prophets did.

Surely, one should always first give food to those who are hungry (1 John 3:17). However, one also has to ask *why* the person is hungry. Does he (or she) not have an income? Does he have no work? Is he unable to work? Have his parents cast him out? Is he the victim of war? Is he the victim of his religion? For instance, the person could be a Hindu who is the poorest of the poor and cannot take up a profession associated with another caste.

The Old Testament prophets were not reluctant to address situations in which widows, orphans, and others were engulfed by distress due to the behavior of greedy and power-hungry people. Old Testament prophets brought accusations against unjust systems (e.g., Isaiah 1:23; Jeremiah 5:28; Hezekiah 22:7; Malachi 3:5) that oppressed the widows in violation of the biblical law, which states, "Do not take advantage of a widow or an orphan" (Exodus 22:22; see also Deuteronomy 24:17; 27:19; Proverbs 23:10; Isaiah 1:17). The Bible says that God "defends the cause of the fatherless and the widow" (Deuteronomy 10:18; Psalm 82:3), which involves more than only providing for them. Jesus complained about the scribes, "They devour widows' houses and for a show make lengthy prayers. Such men will be punished most severely" (Mark 12:40 = Luke 20:47).

63. Human dignity and human rights are founded in the nature of human beings as creatures of God.

The idea of human rights is based on the claim that all people have equal rights to be treated as individuals with dignity, regardless of the differences among them in race, religion, gender, politics, or social and economic status. What is the basis for people's equality, if not the fact that God has made them all equally and with the same dignity? For that reason, every Christian justification for human rights begins with the creation story found in the first two chapters of the Bible. There one reads: "Then God said, 'Let us make man in our image, in our likeness, and let them rule over the fish of the sea and the birds of the air, over the livestock, over all the earth, and over all the creatures that move along the ground.' So God created man in his own image, in the image of God he created him; male and female he created them" (Genesis 1:26–27). An individual's human rights do not depend on whether he or she believes in Jesus Christ or is a Christian; they are conferred simply because that individual has been created.

For that reason, the state does not create human rights, but only formulates and protects them. For example, a human being has the right to life inherently, not because it is bestowed by the state. Thus, the state cannot legitimately decide that its citizens no longer have a right to life. Furthermore, the right to marry and to have a family, mentioned in the Universal Declaration of Human Rights, is not granted by the state, and children and families do not belong to the state. Rather, the state is responsible for protecting the prescribed, created order of marriage and family.

64. Whoever does not actively advocate for society to pursue a good and proper course intentionally or unintentionally accepts the standards of his or her environment.

No person can live without standards and values. Anyone who does not actively take a stand for healthy, just, Christian standards and values in all societies around the world, or who thinks that Christian standards are not even intended for society, has to look for standards somewhere else—

and generally that means looking somewhere in the environment around us.

According to Paul's command, whoever places himself completely in the service of God and who does not want to be conformed to this world, has to continually scrutinize his thinking and have it renewed so that he can test and approve the will of God (Romans 12:1–2).

65. Mission begins in the Christian church and family, where by example, education, and instruction the word of God will be passed on to the next generation.

In addition to proclaiming the Word of God to people outside the church, Christians must not neglect their own families. Having a healthy Christian family is a precondition for all New Testament leadership offices (1 Timothy 3:4–5; 3:12–13; Titus 1:6–7). When Christians give up the rearing of children to others, it hardly makes sense for them to bother with a Christian orientation for the church, the economy, the society, and the state, because they have let the best and most powerful way to mold and transform people for good to be taken out of their control. This emphasis, however, does not contradict the religious freedom of children (Thesis 54).

66. A hope for visible peace grows out of an invisible peace with God in small and in great things, for God desires a future full of peace, in the smallest context of life as well as in worldwide shalom.

Jeremiah 29:11 states, "For I know the plans I have for you," declares the LORD, "plans to prosper you and not to harm you, plans to give you hope and a future." A personal ethic and communal life within a societal framework according to the purposes of Jesus Christ arise out of the peace that an individual experiences with God. And Christians not only receive peace for themselves; they also pass it on and promote it. This is why Jesus says, "Blessed are the meek, for they will inherit the earth" (Matthew 5:5).

Christians wish to live peacefully with adherents of other religions and worldviews and to work with them for the common good and for reconciliation. "If it is possible, as far as it depends on you, live at peace with everyone" (Romans 12:18).

67. Society's destiny is also the destiny that Christians face.

Christians, like everyone else, cannot live without the earth! Indeed, there will one day be a new heaven and a new earth (Revelation 21:1), but even then there will only be human life on an *earth*, just as we hope for eternal life with a new *body* ("heavenly dwelling"), not eternal life without a body (see 2 Corinthians 5:1–8). This is surely not the sole reason why Christians are interested in the destiny of this world and attempt to save what can be saved. However, it is also a biblically legitimate reason, because the future of this world is related to Christians' own future. It is not for their own sake that Christians are concerned about ways in which the world around them may be breaking apart, but so that this world might experience as much peace, justice, and mercy as possible.

Thus God called on the Israelites in pagan Babylon to do good for Babylon, because the destiny of Babylon was the destiny of the people of God: "Also, seek the peace and prosperity of the city to which I have carried you into exile. Pray to the Lord for it, because if it prospers, you too will prosper" (Jeremiah 29:7). In the New Testament, Paul enjoined the church to pray for the government, "that we may live peaceful and quiet lives in all godliness and holiness" (1 Timothy 2:1–3).

In the Sermon on the Mount, Jesus instructed Christians not to place their lamp under a bowl but to become the salt of the earth. Directly after the Beatitudes, using the examples of salt and light, Jesus made it clear that believers should not live and act only for themselves (Matthew 5:13–16). He challenged them to act boldly and openly, on behalf of and in front of all people: "In the same way, let your light shine before men, that they may see your good deeds and praise your Father in heaven" (Matthew 5:16), even if in this connection Christians must also experience ridicule and persecution.

68. Christian hope includes hope for the entire creation, in its consummation as well as in the here-and-now.

The final deliverance of creation encompasses the entire life-filled universe: "For the creation was subjected to frustration, not by its own choice, but by the will of the one who subjected it, in hope" (Romans 8:20; see also verse 24). For that reason, the description of the new heaven and the new earth encompasses a description not only of the people there but also of the earth itself (Revelation 21).

The environmental movement has elevated the safeguarding of creation to its primary agenda. Christians, in contrast, must reaffirm that there is no creation without the Creator and no hope for the creation without hope in the Creator. However, the converse is also true: whoever has hope in the Creator must also have hope for the creation.

Indeed, the dominion that people have been granted over the earth is intended, first and foremost, to serve people. However, it also serves the creation. Whoever holds to God's creation ordinances will, in contrast to godless egoists, work for the benefit of creation: "A righteous man cares for the needs of his animal, but the kindest acts of the wicked are cruel" (Proverbs 12:10). In the creation story, humankind received the mandate to "work" and to "take care" of the world (Genesis 2:15), or both to change and to preserve. In theory, these ideas might sound mutually exclusive, but in everyday life they belong inseparably together. The two types of transformation—changing, renewing, and re-creating on one hand and preserving, strengthening, and protecting on the other hand—belong together like two sides of the same coin.

69. There is hope for the world if the church repents.

Does the Christian church's sense of ultimate hope mean that it should euphorically run after every suggestion for improvement and be blind to how easily good plans are shipwrecked by evil? No. On the contrary, the desired reformation should begin with believers—first with individual renewal and then proceeding to renewal of the family, congregations, and the Church as a whole. "For it is time for judgment to begin with the family of God" (1 Peter 4:17). After all, what Paul said about the Jews in his demonstration that all have sinned is consistent with the Old Testament: "God's name is blasphemed among the Gentiles because of you" (Romans 2:24; cf. Isaiah 52:5). Gottfried Schenkel aptly wrote shortly after World War II, "The judgment which comes upon the world is not only a judgment of dictators, totalitarianism, revolutionary absolutism, and radical pretension. Rather, it is also a judgment that at the same time comes upon Christians on account of their un-Christian-ness, and on account of the weakness of Christians over against other earthly powers."

Therefore, the only way for Christians to work toward renewal of the church and of society is to see what is going wrong from the viewpoint of the word of God and how God desires to have things reordered. We may again recall 2 Chronicles 7:14 at this point: "If my people, who are called by my name, will humble themselves and pray and seek my face and turn from their wicked ways, then will I hear from heaven and will forgive their sin and will heal their land." At that point, the church will truly be able to intercede for the society and the state. Let us hope that what God had to appallingly discern through Ezekiel does not apply to us: "I looked for a man among them who would build up the wall and stand before me in the gap on behalf of the land so I would not have to destroy it, but I found none" (Ezekiel 22:30).

World Evangelical Alliance

World Evangelical Alliance is a global ministry working with local churches around the world to join in common concern to live and proclaim the Good News of Jesus in their communities. WEA is a network of churches in 129 nations that have each formed an evangelical alliance and over 100 international organizations joining together to give a worldwide identity, voice and platform to more than 600 million evangelical Christians. Seeking holiness, justice and renewal at every level of society – individual, family, community and culture, God is glorified and the nations of the earth are forever transformed.

Christians from ten countries met in London in 1846 for the purpose of launching, in their own words, "a new thing in church history, a definite organization for the expression of unity amongst Christian individuals belonging to different churches." This was the beginning of a vision that was fulfilled in 1951 when believers from 21 countries officially formed the World Evangelical Fellowship. Today, 150 years after the London gathering, WEA is a dynamic global structure for unity and action that embraces 600 million evangelicals in 129 countries. It is a unity based on the historic Christian faith expressed in the evangelical tradition. And it looks to the future with vision to accomplish God's purposes in discipling the nations for Jesus Christ.

Commissions:

- Theology
- Missions
- Religious Liberty
- Women's Concerns
- Youth
- Information Technology

Initiatives and Activities

- Ambassador for Human Rights
- Ambassador for Refugees
- Creation Care Task Force
- Global Generosity Network
- International Institute for Religious Freedom
- International Institute for Islamic Studies
- Leadership Institute
- Micah Challenge
- Global Human Trafficking Task Force
- Peace and Reconciliation Initiative
- UN-Team

Church Street Station
P.O. Box 3402
New York, NY 10008-3402
Phone +[1] 212 233 3046
Fax +[1] 646-957-9218
www.worldea.org

WEA
World Evangelical Alliance

Giving Hands

GIVING HANDS GERMANY (GH) was established in 1995 and is officially recognized as a nonprofit foreign aid organization. It is an international operating charity that – up to now – has been supporting projects in about 40 countries on four continents. In particular we care for orphans and street children. Our major focus is on Africa and Central America. GIVING HANDS always mainly provides assistance for self-help and furthers human rights thinking.

The charity itself is not bound to any church, but on the spot we are co-operating with churches of all denominations. Naturally we also cooperate with other charities as well as governmental organizations to provide assistance as effective as possible under the given circumstances.

The work of GIVING HANDS GERMANY is controlled by a supervisory board. Members of this board are Manfred Feldmann, Colonel V. Doner and Kathleen McCall. Dr. Christine Schirrmacher is registered as legal manager of GIVING HANDS at the local district court. The local office and work of the charity are coordinated by Rev. Horst J. Kreie as executive manager. Dr. theol. Thomas Schirrmacher serves as a special consultant for all projects.

Thanks to our international contacts companies and organizations from many countries time and again provide containers with gifts in kind which we send to the different destinations where these goods help to satisfy elementary needs. This statutory purpose is put into practice by granting nutrition, clothing, education, construction and maintenance of training centers at home and abroad, construction of wells and operation of water treatment systems, guidance for self-help and transportation of goods and gifts to areas and countries where needy people live.

GIVING HANDS has a publishing arm under the leadership of Titus Vogt, that publishes human rights and other books in English, Spanish, Swahili and other languages.

These aims are aspired to the glory of the Lord according to the basic Christian principles put down in the Holy Bible.

Baumschulallee 3a • D-53115 Bonn • Germany
Phone: +49 / 228 / 695531 • Fax +49 / 228 / 695532
www.gebende-haende.de • info@gebende-haende.de

Martin Bucer Seminary

Faithful to biblical truth
Cooperating with the Evangelical Alliance
Reformed

Solid training for the Kingdom of God

- Alternative theological education
- Study while serving a church or working another job
- Enables students to remain in their own churches
- Encourages independent thinking
- Learning from the growth of the universal church.

Academic

- For the Bachelor's degree: 180 Bologna-Credits
- For the Master's degree: 120 additional Credits
- Both old and new teaching methods: All day seminars, independent study, term papers, etc.

Our Orientation:

- Complete trust in the reliability of the Bible
- Building on reformation theology
- Based on the confession of the German Evangelical Alliance
- Open for innovations in the Kingdom of God

Our Emphasis:

- The Bible
- Ethics and Basic Theology
- Missions
- The Church

Our Style:

- Innovative
- Relevant to society
- International
- Research oriented
- Interdisciplinary

Structure

- 15 study centers in 7 countries with local partners
- 5 research institutes
- President: Prof. Dr. Thomas Schirrmacher
  Vice President: Prof. Dr. Thomas K. Johnson
- Deans: Thomas Kinker, Th.D.;
  Titus Vogt, lic. theol., Carsten Friedrich, M.Th.

Missions through research

- Institute for Religious Freedom
- Institute for Islamic Studies
- Institute for Life and Family Studies
- Institute for Crisis, Dying, and Grief Counseling
- Institute for Pastoral Care

www.bucer.eu • info@bucer.eu

Berlin | Bielefeld | Bonn | Chemnitz | Hamburg | Munich | Pforzheim
Innsbruck | Istanbul | Izmir | Linz | Prague | São Paulo | Tirana | Zurich

www.ingramcontent.com/pod-product-compliance
Lightning Source LLC
LaVergne TN
LVHW051709080426
835511LV00017B/2814